OECD Economic Surveys: Ireland 2015

This document and any map included herein are without prejudice to the status of or sovereignty over any territory, to the delimitation of international frontiers and boundaries and to the name of any territory, city or area.

Please cite this publication as:
OECD (2015), *OECD Economic Surveys: Ireland 2015*, OECD Publishing, Paris.
http://dx.doi.org/10.1787/eco_surveys-irl-2015-en

ISBN 978-92-64-24032-2 (print)
ISBN 978-92-64-24033-9 (PDF)
ISBN 978-92-64-24059-9 (epub)

Series: OECD Economic Surveys
ISSN 0376-6438 (print)
ISSN 1609-7513 (online)

OECD Economic Surveys: Ireland
ISSN 1995-3267 (print)
ISSN 1999-0324 (online)

The statistical data for Israel are supplied by and under the responsibility of the relevant Israeli authorities. The use of such data by the OECD is without prejudice to the status of the Golan Heights, East Jerusalem and Israeli settlements in the West Bank under the terms of international law.

Photo credits: Cover © Paul Campbell/Shutterstock.com.

Corrigenda to OECD publications may be found on line at: *www.oecd.org/about/publishing/corrigenda.htm*.

© OECD 2015

You can copy, download or print OECD content for your own use, and you can include excerpts from OECD publications, databases and multimedia products in your own documents, presentations, blogs, websites and teaching materials, provided that suitable acknowledgement of OECD as source and copyright owner is given. All requests for public or commercial use and translation rights should be submitted to *rights@oecd.org*. Requests for permission to photocopy portions of this material for public or commercial use shall be addressed directly to the Copyright Clearance Center (CCC) at *info@copyright.com* or the Centre français d'exploitation du droit de copie (CFC) at *contact@cfcopies.com*.

Table of contents

Thematic chapters

Tables

Figures

This Survey is published on the responsibility of the Economic and Development Review Committee of the OECD, which is charged with the examination of the economic situation of member countries.

The Economic situation and policies of Ireland were reviewed by the Committee on 9 July 2015. The draft was revised in the light of the discussion and given final approval as the agreed report of the whole Committee on 28 July 2015.

The Secretariat's draft report was prepared for the Committee by David Haugh, Yosuke Jin, Alberto Gonzales Pandiella and Muge Adalet Mcgowan under the supervision of Patrick Lenain. Damien Azzopardi, Penelope Silice and Elika Athari provided the statistical research assistance, and Brigitte Beyeler, Mikel Inarritu and Anthony Bolton provided the administrative support.

The previous Survey of Ireland was issued in September 2013.

Follow OECD Publications on:

 *http://twitter.com/OECD_Pubs*

 *http://www.facebook.com/OECDPublications*

 *http://www.linkedin.com/groups/OECD-Publications-4645871*

http://www.youtube.com/oecdilibrary

http://www.oecd.org/oecddirect/

This book has...

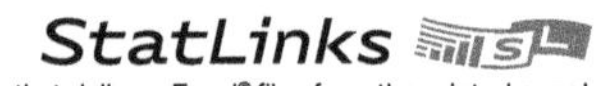

A service that delivers Excel® files from the printed page!

Look for the *StatLinks* at the bottom of the tables or graphs in this book. To download the matching Excel® spreadsheet, just type the link into your Internet browser, starting with the *http://dx.doi.org* prefix, or click on the link from the e-book edition.

BASIC STATISTICS OF IRELAND, 2014

(Numbers in parentheses refer to the OECD average)*

LAND, PEOPLE AND ELECTORAL CYCLE					
Population (million)	4.6		Population density per km²	65.6	(34.9)
Under 15 (%)	22.0	(18.1)	Life expectancy (years, 2013)	81.1	(80.5)
Over 65 (%)	12.7	(16.0)	Men	79.0	(77.8)
Foreign-born (%, 2011)	16.4		Women	83.1	(83.1)
Latest 5-year average growth (%)	0.3	(0.6)	Latest general election	February 2011	
ECONOMY					
Gross domestic product (GDP)			Value added shares (%, 2013)		
In current prices (billion USD)	251.1		Primary sector	1.6	(2.6)
In current prices (billion EUR)	189.0		Industry including construction	24.1	(26.5)
Latest 5-year average real growth (%)	1.9	(1.9)	Services	74.3	(71.0)
Per capita (000 USD PPP)	48.8	(39.0)			
GENERAL GOVERNMENT Per cent of GDP					
Expenditure[a]	38.3	(41.9)	Gross financial debt[a]	107.6	(112.1)
Revenue[a]	34.2	(37.8)	Net financial debt[a]	81.8	(69.0)
EXTERNAL ACCOUNTS					
Exchange rate (EUR per USD)	0.753		Main exports (% of total merchandise exports)		
PPP exchange rate (USA = 1)	0.841		Chemicals and related products, n.e.s.		57.8
In per cent of GDP			Miscellaneous manufactured articles		12.8
Exports of goods and services	113.7	(53.7)	Machinery and transport equipment		11.2
Imports of goods and services	95.4	(49.6)	Main imports (% of total merchandise imports)		
Current account balance	6.1	(0.0)	Machinery and transport equipment		27.0
Net international investment position (2013)	-100.2		Chemicals and related products, n.e.s.		21.2
			Miscellaneous manufactured articles		12.7
LABOUR MARKET, SKILLS AND INNOVATION					
Employment rate for 15-64 year-olds (%)	61.7	(65.7)	Unemployment rate, Labour Force Survey (age 15 and over) (%)	11.3	(7.3)
Men	66.9	(73.6)	Youth (age 15-24, %)	23.9	(15.0)
Women	56.7	(57.9)	Long-term unemployed (1 year and over, %)	6.6	(2.5)
Participation rate for 15-64 year-olds (%)	69.7	(71.2)	Tertiary educational attainment 25-64 year-olds (%, 2013)	41.5	(33.3)
Average hours worked per year	1 821	(1 770)	Gross domestic expenditure on R&D (% of GDP, 2012[a])	1.6	(2.4)
ENVIRONMENT					
Total primary energy supply per capita (toe, 2013)	2.9	(4.2)	CO_2 emissions from fuel combustion per capita (tonnes, 2012)	7.8	(9.7)
Renewables (%, 2013)	6.2	(8.8)	Municipal waste per capita (tonnes, 2012)	0.6	(0.5)
Fine particulate matter concentration (urban, PM10, µg/m³, 2011)	17.8	(28.0)			
SOCIETY					
Income inequality (Gini coefficient, 2012)	0.304	(0.308)	Ratio of incomes of the top 10% vs. bottom 10%, 2012	7.4	(9.6)
Relative poverty rate (%, 2012)	8.4	(10.9)	Education outcomes (PISA score, 2012)		
Median disposable household income (000 USD PPP, 2012)	22.0	(21.9)	Reading	523	(496)
Public and private spending (% of GDP)			Mathematics	501	(494)
Health care (2012[a])	8.1	(9.0)	Science	522	(501)
Pensions (2011)	5.8	(8.7)	Share of women in parliament (%, August 2015)	19.9	(26.0)
Education (primary, secondary, post sec. non tertiary, 2011)	4.6	(3.9)	Net official development assistance (% of GNI)	0.39	(0.36)

Better life index: *www.oecdbetterlifeindex.org*

a) 2013 for the OECD aggregate.

* Where the OECD aggregate is not provided in the source database, a simple OECD average of latest available data is calculated where data exist for at least 29 member countries.

Source: Calculations based on data extracted from the databases of the following organisations: OECD, International Energy Agency, World Bank, International Monetary Fund and Inter-Parliamentary Union.

© OECD 2015

Executive summary

- *Main findings*
- *Key recommendations*

Strong economic growth has returned to Ireland

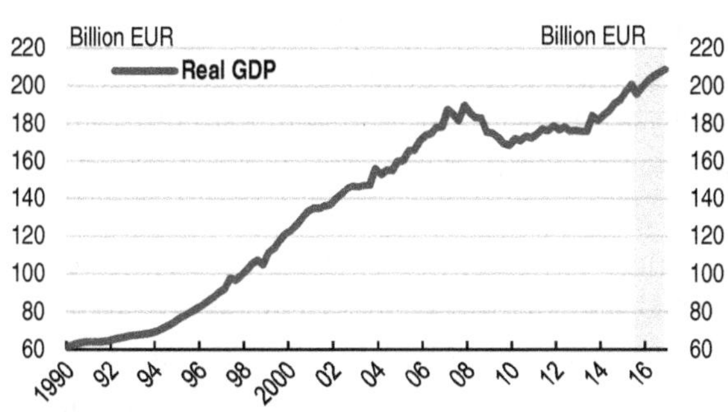

Source: CSO and OECD *Economic Outlook 97 Database*, projections revised as of 10 September 2015.

StatLink http://dx.doi.org/10.1787/888933274998

Determined policy efforts have boosted confidence and underpinned the robust, broad-based recovery now underway in Ireland. Unemployment is falling steadily, the budget deficit is declining, public debt has peaked and continues to fall and international credibility has been strengthened. These propitious circumstances are the opportunity to resolve the legacies of the crisis, including remaining unemployment and banking system weaknesses. There is also a chance to carry out structural reforms to ensure the recovery is sustained. Real estate prices, especially in commercial and residential property in Dublin, are rising rapidly once again, and pressures to narrow the tax base and increase spending are growing.

Welfare transfers have narrowed income gaps but more needs to be done to get people into work

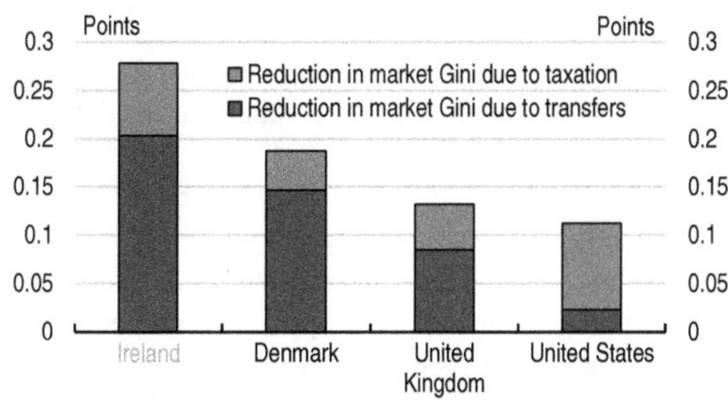

Source: Provisional data from *OECD Income Distribution Database*, latest data.

StatLink http://dx.doi.org/10.1787/888933275001

During the crisis, Ireland's comprehensive welfare system supported demand, underpinned social cohesion and provided a sense of fairness that made needed reforms possible. However, highly targeted benefits including housing benefit result in high replacement rates and marginal effective tax rates for some households at the low end of the income distribution, discouraging work. The solution is to intensify activation policies to get people into jobs, improve training and enforce obligations on benefit recipients to seek a job or take training.

Productivity growth remains modest, hindering long-term prospects

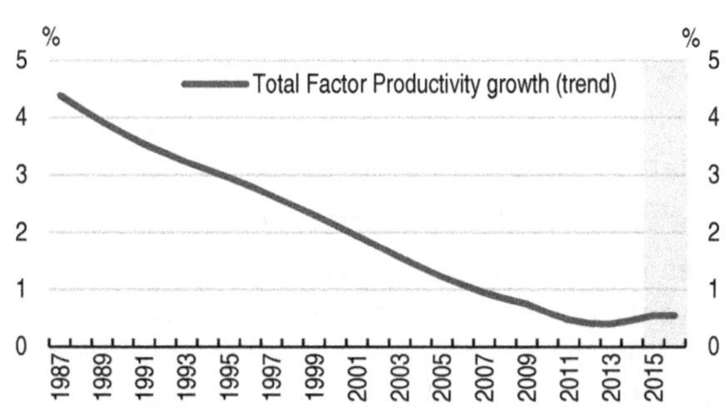

Source: OECD *Economic Outlook Database*.

StatLink http://dx.doi.org/10.1787/888933275011

Productivity growth has been falling for some time. Although Ireland's multinational sector thrived through the crisis, the domestic SME sector is still lagging behind despite the shift away from the low productivity construction sector, with much lower levels of competitiveness, productivity and R&D spending. Strengthening competition in sectors including legal services and ports, further improving the regulatory environment for business and encouraging innovation are all policy priorities.

MAIN FINDINGS	KEY RECOMMENDATIONS
Fiscal sustainability	
The fiscal position has improved and public debt is on a declining path. However, the budget deficit remains too large and spending pressures are rising.	Improve the structural fiscal balance by greater than 0.5% of GDP per annum until it reaches balance. Allow the automatic stabilisers to work around this path.
	Improve health spending efficiency including by fully implementing "money follows the patient" in health spending and publishing improved indicators of financial and operational performances of hospitals.
	Broaden and protect the tax base by shifting the burden of taxation to immovable assets, reducing allowances for capital income and continue aligning the corporate income tax system, including its transfer pricing rules, with recommendations from the OECD/G20 BEPS project.
Financial stability	
The repossession of collateral on non-performing loans is inefficient.	Accelerate through the court system the resolution of non-performing loans that require repossessions
Recent rises in property prices pose risks.	Continue to improve the responsiveness of housing supply including in the rental market and avoid home buyer subsidies.
Inclusive growth	
Skill mismatches are high. Reducing them would lower unemployment and increase both participation and productivity significantly.	Step up efforts to develop and implement a more agile, relevant, and gender inclusive apprenticeship system. Ensure that students receive information on education options after schooling, notably vocational and technical options.
Education outcomes depend on social background and concentration of immigrants in primary schools is increasing. The DEIS (Delivering Equality of opportunity In Schools) programme has experienced significant budget cuts in recent years.	Provide additional support to disadvantaged schools, for example by attracting better teachers and providing additional tutoring to students
Long-term unemployment is high and labour-market participation is low among those with low levels of education, and among women over 30.	Upskill long-term unemployed by improving both the quantity and quality of training via public employment services or via private providers.
	Fully enforce the obligations of the unemployed and improve the enforcement framework by defining more objectively the suitable job offer that the benefit recipient has to accept in terms of wages and contract types.
	Improve access and affordability of quality childcare, particularly for low income families.

MAIN FINDINGS	KEY RECOMMENDATIONS
Rapid withdrawal of housing assistance payments and the family income supplement result in very high replacement and marginal effective tax rates for particular low-paid households.	To reduce welfare traps, more gradually reduce housing assistance payments and family income supplement as income increases.
Productivity	
Public support for business R&D is increasingly skewed towards R&D tax credits	Rebalance innovation support towards direct grants.
Ireland relies on highly skilled workers with specific abilities. Migrants can play an important role in that respect.	Make better use of international students as a channel for high-skill immigration by increasing post-graduation job search periods and exempting graduates from employment permit fees in highly demanded areas where there are significant skills shortages.
Many government agencies devise policies to improve business sector performance, but without the proper research capacity and independence to advocate reforms and engage in a dialogue with stakeholders.	Develop a stronger whole-of-government productivity agenda. Consider expanding the remit of the National Competitiveness Council into a more productivity-focussed body.
Environmental sustainability	
Household water quality fails Environmental Protection Agency standards in some areas and there are excessive water leakages.	Increase investment to improve water quality and reduce leakages.
Increasing housing energy efficiency is a cheap way to reduce GHG emissions.	Increase support to improve the energy efficiency of housing, especially for low-income households.

© OECD 2015

Assessment and recommendations

- *Macroeconomic performance and risks*
- *Further strengthening the fiscal position*
- *Ensuring financial stability*
- *Making growth more inclusive*
- *Fostering productivity*
- *Improving environmental sustainability*

Following a property-led boom, Ireland was hit by a severe banking and fiscal crisis in 2008. Determined policy implementation has restored confidence and underpinned the strong cyclical recovery now underway (Figure 1).

Ireland has come a long way in the past 5 years since it entered the EU-IMF financial assistance programme. Determined reform efforts by the government, both under the auspices of the programme and subsequently, have paid off. Ireland has emerged from the crisis with a much reduced and still declining fiscal deficit, public debt on a downward path, a stronger fiscal framework, a more sustainable fiscal revenue base, a restructured and recapitalised banking sector, a strengthened and more efficient public administration, and a much improved labour market activation regime (Table 1, Annex). This has been rewarded by renewed access to financial market borrowing for both banks and the sovereign.

Ireland successfully exited the financial assistance programme in December 2013. An important contributor to the success of the programme was strong ownership by Ireland itself. The government had already undertaken significant consolidation action in 2009-10. In addition, the programme was largely based on the 2010 Irish government's *National Recovery Plan 2011-2014*, with modifications introduced by the current government in 2011. Other factors were a committed public administration capable of delivering a large number of complex reforms quickly, supported by the Croke Park agreement, which contributed to industrial peace in the public sector. Also important was the underlying structural strengths of Ireland that continued to attract and benefit from foreign investment throughout the crisis.

Figure 1. **Strong growth is returning to Ireland**

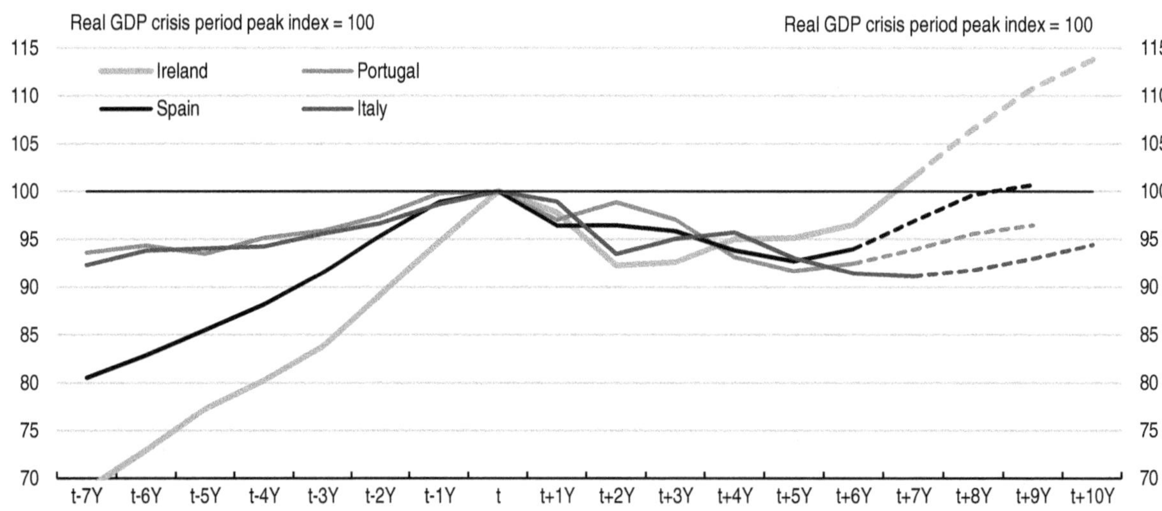

Note: Peak date for Ireland and Spain is 2007, 2008 for Italy and Portugal.
Source: OECD, *Analytical Database* and OECD calculations.

StatLink http://dx.doi.org/10.1787/888933275027

Table 1. **Progress on structural reforms**

Reform	Main Legislation Enacted	New or empowered regulator	Remaining steps to be taken
Fiscal	December 2012	Yes	...
Financial and banking	October 2010 and August 2013	Yes	...
Personal insolvency	December 2013	Yes	...
Competition	July 2014	Yes	...
Legal profession	No	Intended	...
Corporate governance	December 2014	No	
Water	March 2013	Yes	Complete the roll-out of household water meters
Labour market activation	No legislation. Pathways to Work Reforms start February 2012	Yes	Full roll-out of contracting out of job-search services
Further education and training	October 2013	Yes	Design and implement new apprenticeships and vocational training.
Government accountability and transparency	July 2013, July and October 2014	Yes	
Health (pharmaceuticals pricing)	May 2013	Yes	

Source: OECD and *Irish Statute Book.*

Key structural reforms have also been rolled out. The government's *Action Plan for Jobs* provides momentum for designing and implementing a coherent set of labour-market reforms and should continue. Ireland has also strengthened its institutional framework, with a new independent fiscal council, fiscal rules, reformed public employment service and activation policies, a vocational training authority, a stronger competition authority, a new agency to facilitate knowledge transfer, and increased transparency and openness in government. These welcome reforms will have long-lasting pay-offs but Ireland should be careful to avoid complacency.

Ireland now faces three main challenges:

- enhancing its economic resilience by moving towards a balanced budget in structural terms to reduce the high public debt, and by strengthening the banking system;
- making growth more inclusive by increasing labour market participation while further reducing unemployment, particularly long-term unemployment; and
- improving long-term growth prospects by making the Irish-owned business sector more dynamic, productive and innovative, while maintaining attractiveness to foreign investment.

Macroeconomic performance and risks

The Irish economy is strongly rebounding from the crisis, with GDP growth of 5.2% in 2014, the fastest in the OECD. In part, this reflected temporary factors such as the fading of the patent cliff (the expiry of a number of drug patents), which weighed on exports in 2013. The initial stages of the recovery was largely driven by multi-national companies (MNCs) that account for a large share of production in sectors that are less sensitive to cyclical fluctuations, such as pharmaceuticals and medical devices.

Consistent with the performance of the MNCs, export growth has been strong, as Ireland has gained market share thanks partly to improved cost-competitiveness since 2009 (Figure 2). Labour costs adjusted swiftly after the onset of the crisis. Relative unit labour costs (labour costs adjusted for productivity and compared with Ireland's trading partners) declined by around 15% by end-2010. Part of this reflected a shift to higher

Figure 2. **Regained competitiveness contributes to Irish exports**

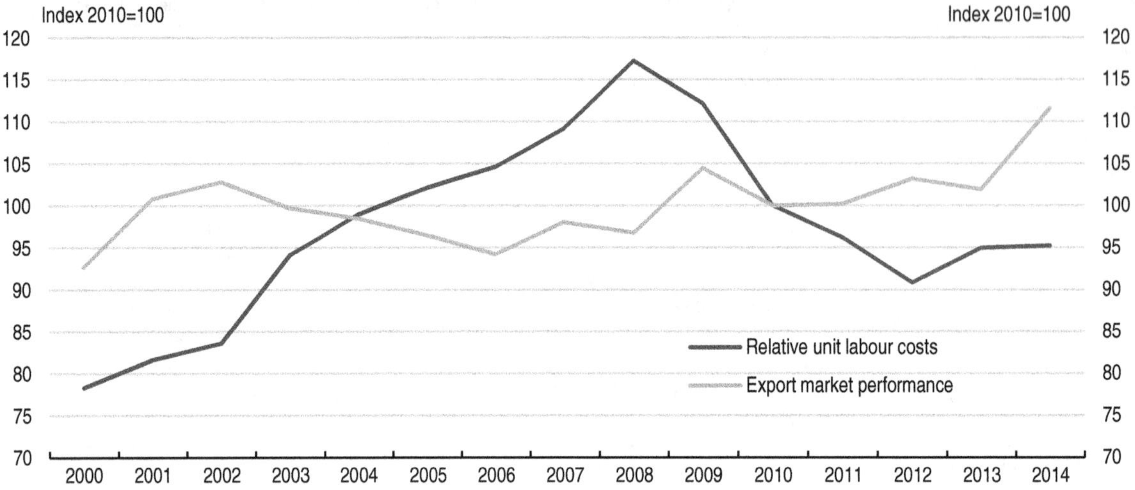

Source: OECD, *OECD Economic Outlook Database.*

StatLink http://dx.doi.org/10.1787/888933275037

productivity sectors (O'Farrell, 2015), but controlling for this relative unit labour costs still fell by 8.4% over the same period (O'Brien and Scally, 2012). The current account balance has reversed significantly from -5.7% of GDP in 2008 to 6.1% of GDP in 2014, although partly because of the profits of foreign companies with activities elsewhere but headquartered in Ireland (Fitzgerald, 2013).

Employment has expanded steadily since 2012 (Figure 3) and unemployment has declined substantially. As a consequence, wage growth has more recently regained some strength. Together with lower inflation, this has led to the growth of household disposable real income turning positive in 2014 for the first time in several years. However, the long-term unemployed and those outside the labour market still account for a larger share of the working-age population than before the crisis or in other OECD countries.

Balance-sheet repair in the banking sector has progressed in recent years and the overall financial situation has improved. The banking sector returned to profitability in 2014, after making losses for several years, mainly due to a reduction in impairment charges. Nevertheless, private-sector (households and non-financial corporations) debt is still high at 290% of GDP, well above the euro area average of about 165% (Figure 4). In addition, non-performing loans still account for just under a fifth of the value of outstanding loans (Figure 4), although this includes some restructured loans. The value of non-performing loans (NPL) peaked at just under EUR 100 billion in mid-2013 but the NPL ratio continued to rise through to 2013Q4 due to the declining loan stock, peaking at 25.7%. The share of very long-term mortgage arrears (720 days and over) in total arrears is still increasing albeit at a much slower rate.

The economy is projected to grow by around 5% in 2015 and 4% in 2016. Growth is projected to broaden with more balanced contributions from exports and domestic demand (Table 2). Macroeconomic policy is becoming more stimulatory owing to less fiscal consolidation and the ECB's quantitative easing policy. Exports will continue to be strong due to increasing demand in trading partners, notably the United States and the United

Figure 3. **The recovery is well underway and becoming more broad-based**

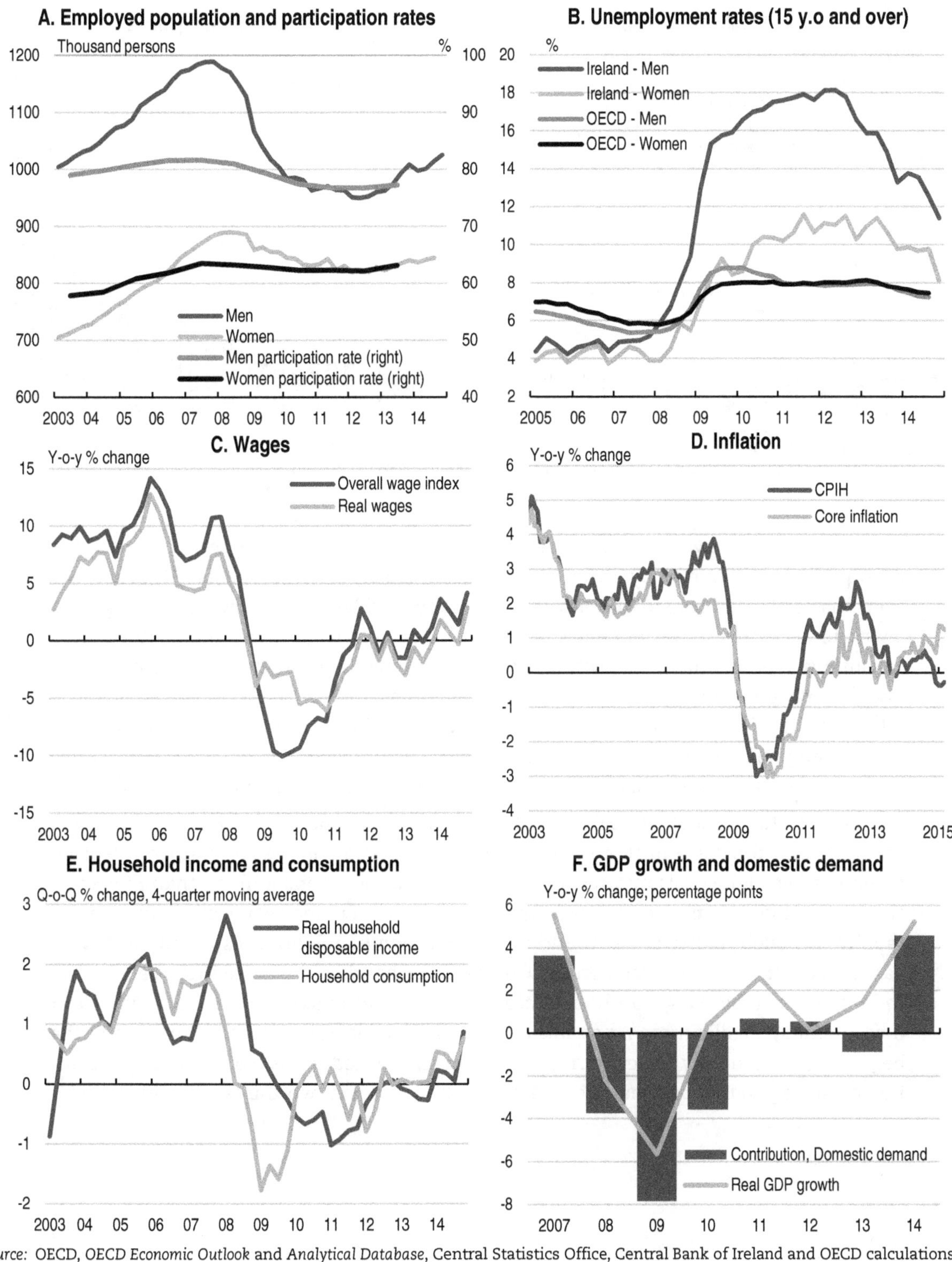

Source: OECD, *OECD Economic Outlook* and *Analytical Database*, Central Statistics Office, Central Bank of Ireland and OECD calculations.

StatLink http://dx.doi.org/10.1787/888933275047

Figure 4. **Debt and non-performing loans are high**

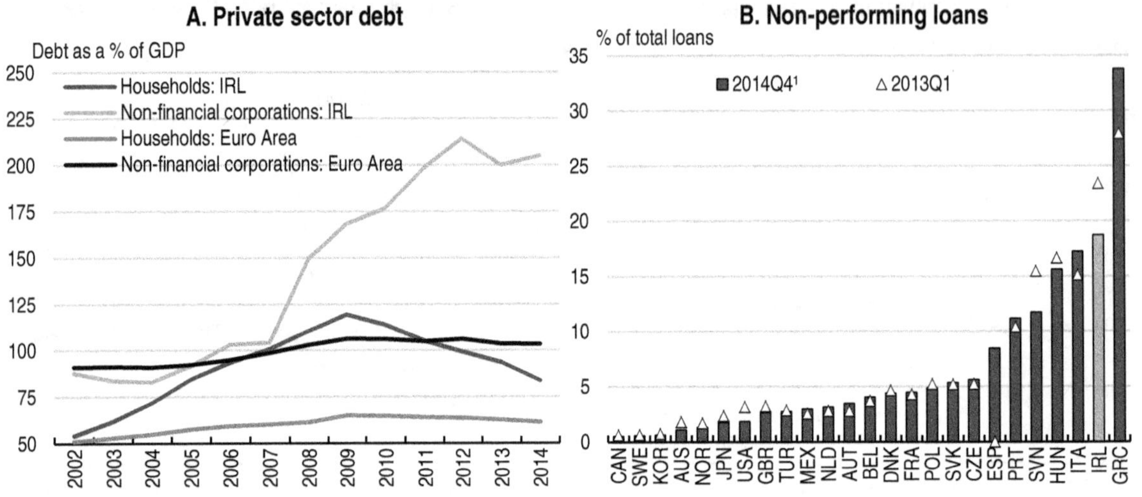

A. Private sector debt

B. Non-performing loans

1. 2014Q4 or latest data available.

Source: Central Statistics Office; Central Bank of Ireland, and IMF, *Financial Soundness Indicators.*

StatLink http://dx.doi.org/10.1787/888933275057

Kingdom, and to the weaker euro. Investment will grow solidly as the investment-to-GDP ratio picks up supported by an improvement in profitability prospects. Although the transmission mechanism to the euro area periphery is still impaired, lower financing costs owing to accommodative monetary policy will also help to lift investment. Household consumption will gather pace, with stronger wage growth and higher employment; and lower energy prices will boost purchasing power in the short run. Banks, weighed down by a large stock of unprofitable tracker mortgages, are likely to cross-subsidise them by maintaining variable mortgage interest rates for new mortgages far above ECB policy rates in a bid to stay profitable. This may impede new credit growth and household mobility.

Risks to the outlook are balanced. On the one hand, the recovery of the euro area economy may provide a further boost to Irish exports and business investment. Pent-up demand after a long crisis may result in stronger household consumption than projected. Housing investment may accelerate faster than expected if property prices continue to rise rapidly, although higher prices would also increase vulnerabilities, especially if it were associated with further indebtedness. On the other hand, still elevated joblessness and indebtedness may weigh on household spending and constrained credit may limit investment by smaller firms. A possible increase in financial turmoil in the euro area or the beginning of monetary policy normalisation in the United States could be harmful for Ireland since public debt remains over 100% of GDP, of which two-thirds are held abroad.

Table 2. **Macroeconomic indicators and projections**

Annual percentage change, volume (2013 prices)

	2011 Current prices (billion EUR)	2012	2013	2014	2015	2016
Gross domestic product (GDP)	173.9	0.1	1.4	5.2	5.0	4.0
Private consumption	79.6	-1.0	0.1	2.1	2.9	3.1
Government consumption	31.1	-1.3	-0.1	4.0	4.0	1.6
Gross fixed capital formation	29.8	8.6	-6.2	14.0	15.1	7.7
Housing	3.5	-20.6	5.0	-3.5	9.0	8.7
Business		..	..	..	..	..
Government		..	..	..	..	..
Final domestic demand	140.5	0.8	-1.5	5.1	6.1	4.0
Stockbuilding[1]	2.0	-0.2	0.3	0.5	0.0	0.0
Total domestic demand	142.6	1.0	-1.2	5.6	5.9	3.9
Exports of goods and services	176.1	2.1	2.5	12.1	11.9	4.6
Imports of goods and services	144.8	2.9	0.0	14.7	13.3	4.4
Net exports[1]	31.3	-0.3	2.7	0.1	0.9	1.1
Other indicators (growth rates, unless specified)						
Potential GDP	..	1.2	0.9	1.3	1.8	1.9
Output gap[2]	..	-5.9	-5.4	-1.8	1.2	3.2
Employment	..	-0.6	2.3	1.8	2.2	2.5
Unemployment rate	..	14.7	13.0	11.3	9.6	8.4
GDP deflator	..	0.4	1.2	0.1	3.1	2.0
Consumer price index (harmonised)	..	1.9	0.5	0.3	0.0	1.6
Core consumer prices (harmonised)	..	0.7	0.1	0.7	1.6	1.7
Household saving ratio, net[3]	..	7.8	7.1	6.3	6.6	7.5
Trade balance[4]	..	-1.6	-14.7	26.8	..	..
Current account balance[4]	..	1.5	4.3	6.1	4.2	3.9
Three-month money market rate, average	..	0.6	0.2	0.2	0.0	0.0
Ten-year government bond yield, average	..	6.0	3.8	2.3	1.1	1.3

1. Contribution to changes in real GDP.
2. As a percentage of potential GDP.
3. As a percentage of household disposable income.
4. As a percentage of GDP.

Source: OECD (2015), *OECD Economic Outlook 97 Database*, projections revised as of 10 September 2015.

Further strengthening the fiscal position

Ireland needs to keep improving the fiscal position to face the next downturn in the world economy. A more robust fiscal position is particularly important because monetary policy is not independent, and private and public sector indebtedness remains high, making Ireland more vulnerable to negative shocks. Ireland has steadily ameliorated its fiscal position in recent years, and this is projected to continue (Table 3). Between 2009 and 2014, the fiscal deficit (excluding bank-related financial measures) fell from 11.5% to 4.0% of GDP, while gross public debt fell from 120.1% of GDP in 2013 to 107.6% in 2014, mainly due to the winding up of IBRC (formerly Anglo-Irish Bank) and as a result net debt did not decline. Ireland's high public debt pushed gross interest costs up from 1% in 2007 to 4% of GDP in 2014. Debt payments would have been greater had Ireland not negotiated improvements in the structure of its sovereign debt.

To keep improving the fiscal position debt needs to be maintained on a firmly declining path over the medium-term. Simulations using the OECD's long-term baseline projections for growth show that eliminating the budget deficit in line with EU fiscal rules

Table 3. **Fiscal indicators**

General government, as a percentage of GDP or potential GDP

	2011	2012	2013	2014	2015[1]	2016[1]
Fiscal balance	-12.5	-8.0	-5.7	-4.0	-2.2	-1.7
Total revenue	33.0	33.8	34.0	34.2	33.5	32.9
Total expenditure	45.5	41.8	39.6	38.3	35.7	34.6
Underlying primary fiscal balance[2]	-3.8	-2.0	-0.5	-0.2	-0.2	-0.7
Underlying fiscal balance	-6.3	-6.3	-5.0	-3.8	-3.7	-3.5
Fiscal one-offs	-3.5	0.0	0.9	0.5	0.7	0.7
Gross interest payments	3.4	4.1	4.3	4.0	3.6	3.4
Gross debt (Maastricht)	109.3	120.3	120.1	107.6	103.7	99.9
Net debt	60.1	78.5	81.5	81.8	77.8	75.1

1. Projections.
2. Net of cyclical effects and one-offs.

Source: OECD (2015), *OECD Economic Outlook 97 Database*, projections revised as of 10 September 2015.

will put public debt on a declining path and is therefore an appropriate strategy (Figure 5). While the Irish Fiscal Advisory Council (IFAC) suggests that the government's plan for 2016 in the Stability Programme Update 2015 falls short of the requirements of the Preventive Arm of the EU Stability and Growth Pact (IFAC, 2015), the European Commission has assessed the Stability programme as fully compliant with the Pact. The pace of debt reduction is sensitive to the amount of deficit reduction and GDP growth, and the Irish economy is subject to several medium-term uncertainties (Box 1). The government should ensure that Budget 2016 is fully in line with its own rules and EU obligations. It should also

Figure 5. **Balancing the budget would put debt on a downward trend**

General government gross debt, percentage of GDP

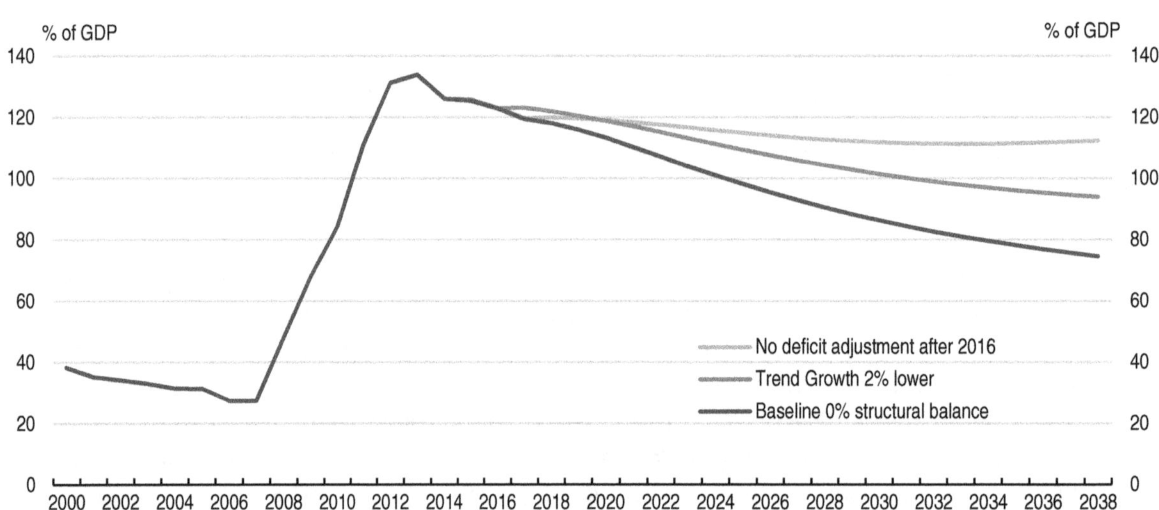

Note: All scenarios use the projections in the Economic Outlook Database No. 97 for the years 2015 and 2016. In the baseline scenario, trend GDP growth averages 1.8% per annum from 2017 to 2040 and the fiscal balance reaches 0% of GDP in 2021 and stays there. In the no deficit adjustment scenario trend GDP growth averages 1.8% per annum from 2017 to 2040 and the fiscal balance remains at -2.8% of GDP in 2017 and beyond. In the trend growth 2% lower scenario, trend GDP growth averages -0.2% from 2017 to 2040 and the fiscal deficit moves to 0% by 2022, where it remains.

Source: *OECD Economic Outlook Database* No. 97; OECD calculations.

StatLink http://dx.doi.org/10.1787/888933275066

Box 1. **Uncertainties about the Irish economy's prospects**

Uncertainty	Possible outcome
Medium-term growth	The world economy may experience lower trend growth over the medium term that would affect Ireland strongly given its openness in trade and financial transactions. As a result, the Irish economy may stagnate given still high joblessness, high indebtedness and large amount of non-performing loans. Should inflation remain very low, these problems would become more difficult to be resolved. However, productivity growth could surprise on the upside given its recent modest pace.
Property boom and bust	House prices, though well below their peak level, have increased strongly since their trough in early 2013 and commercial property prices are climbing sharply. Such strong price rises may again spark a reinforcing spiral of higher property prices and credit leading to another misalignment of property prices and eventual burst that causes large losses in the banking sector.
Changes in the international tax regime	Fiscal harmonisation or other changes at EU or OECD level on Ireland's corporation tax regime could have a significant economy-wide impact[1]
Contagion from euro area turmoil	Notwithstanding the institutional improvements in the euro area, any re-emergence of the banking and sovereign crisis could have negative implications for Ireland.
Uncertainty regarding the nature of the economic relationship between the United Kingdom and the European Union	Trade and investment links are very strong, especially for more labour intensive domestic exporters. This presents both opportunities and challenges.

1. Department of the Taoiseach, 2015.

adhere to its obligations to have a robust medium-term fiscal framework including more detailed projections that incorporate demographic and other spending pressures.

To strengthen the fiscal position the government should: allow the automatic stabilisers to operate and put extra revenue from growth above trend into debt reduction; put all the gains of the fall in interest rates to well below the long-run average towards reducing the debt burden faster; increase the robustness of revenue by broadening the tax base; and continue to improve the expenditure control framework, especially for big ticket items including health spending and public sector wage costs, which have grown too quickly in the past. As discussed below broadening the tax base should be accompanied by lowering of high effective marginal tax rates on labour that impede the incentive to work. These marginal rates could be lowered at the bottom end of the income distribution in a broadly fiscally neutral way by introducing a third lower income tax band, lowering the bottom rates of the universal social charge and reducing large tax credits (Chapter 1).

The government in a welcome move introduced a local property tax in 2013 but revenue from property taxes remains low by international standards. The base broadening should include further increasing recurrent property taxation, which is less growth distorting than other taxes (Johansson et al., 2008). Home ownership is widespread across all the income deciles in Ireland and therefore raising property taxes would be regressive. However, it can be done in a way that protects those on lower incomes, albeit at the cost of some increase in administrative complexity and very mildly increasing marginal effective tax rates on labour (O'Connor et al., 2015).

The government could also broaden the tax base by further reducing tax allowances and exemptions. Capital income allowances and exemptions mainly benefit higher income households, which receive the majority of this income (Kennedy et al., 2015). The reduction of taxation related to superannuation is among the more expensive tax expenditures. Reduced VAT rates are costly and inefficient way to address inequality challenges.

There has also been over reliance on bulk grants to cover hospital costs, resulting in overruns in hospitals where activity levels rise and resources wasted in areas with declining demand. In a welcome move, the government began to introduce activity-based funding for the health sector (money follows the patient) in 2014. The moratorium on hiring has now been appropriately replaced with a ceiling on personnel expenditure, which allows hospitals greater flexibility to manage human resources. This should reduce the practice of hiring expensive temps to get around headcount restrictions. To better assess spending efficiency, the government should follow through on its plans to create, and publish, data on the financial and operational performance of hospitals.

After extremely strong wage growth in the boom years, wages and pensions for public servants were cut, and strong public sector wage control secured, under the Financial Emergency Measures in the Public Interest Acts 2009-2013. These were underpinned by industrial relations agreements with public service unions covering the years 2010-14 (Croke Park), 2013-16 (Haddington Road) and 2015-18 (Lansdowne Road) under which, in exchange for public sector efficiency improvements, the government agreed with unions to no further comprehensive wage cuts or compulsory redundancies. The government has recently agreed to begin the process of gradually reducing the cuts applied during this period from 2016. While the agreement is within budgetary parameters, the move raises a concern that, in the absence of appropriate structures for wage determination that take into account issues such as competitiveness, pressure for excessive public sector wage increases could return.

Ensuring financial stability

In response to the 2008 banking crisis and the burst of the housing bubble, the authorities consolidated financial regulation in the central bank, adopting more risk-based and intrusive supervision, transferred large bad property loans to NAMA (a "bad bank"), and undertook capital injections, liquidity support and government guarantees (see the *2011 OECD Economic Survey*). In addition, Ireland introduced a special resolution regime for banks, strengthened the deposit insurance scheme, issued a code of conduct to address mortgage arrears, and reformed the personal bankruptcy regime (see the *2013 OECD Economic Survey*). Since November 2014, the EU Single Supervisor Mechanism (SSM) has had the main responsibility for regulatory and supervision issues, but implementation remains mostly in the hands of the national regulators.

Banks are now well capitalised by international standards and, at 14.5% in March 2015 the average core Tier 1 capital ratio of domestic banks is high. The European Central Bank's Comprehensive Assessment in late 2014 confirmed a small capital shortfall in only one bank, which has since been addressed. The financial supervisor should continue to monitor banks' progress in meeting the forthcoming Capital Requirements Regulation (CRR), which along with the Capital Requirements Directive (CRD) IV implements Basel III rules in the EU, as some instruments now included in capital, such as deferred tax assets and preference shares, will be excluded. A recent review found that excluding these instruments would reduce the aggregate core Tier 1 capital ratio for domestic banks from 15.3% to 7.9% although all banks would remain above the 4.5% minimum requirements under CRD IV (Central Bank of Ireland, 2015). Banks also returned to profitability in the first half of 2014, mainly due to a reduction in the flow of new provisions. However, profitability remains relatively low and low levels of new lending and limited scope to increase lending margins will restrict the ability of banks to increase their income.

While market funding has improved, over half of the funding of the domestic banking system has a maturity of less than one month. While the share of on-demand deposits of non-financial corporations is just below the euro area average, it's above the euro area average for households and the central bank should encourage the banks to increase the maturity of household deposits. Banks will have to improve their funding structure to meet the forthcoming liquidity requirements of the CRR, which may present some challenges (Central Bank of Ireland, 2014). In a welcome move, the authorities now report liquidity positions of large individual banks in financial stability reports, as is the case in other OECD countries, enhancing transparency.

Non-performing loans (NPLs) are high in an international context (18.7% of loans at end-2014; Figure 4), although banks hold provisions against around 50% of them. In April 2015, the Central Bank introduced new requirements to conclude sustainable solutions for a majority of distressed mortgages by the end of 2015. However, resolving some mortgages in long-term arrears will require repossessions if they cannot be restructured in a way that would be acceptable to both debtor and creditor. Repossession proceedings can take a considerable amount of time mainly due to requests from parties for adjournments – in 2015 to date the average time taken from the issue of proceedings to the granting of a Possession Order is approximately 53 weeks. New Rules of Court (which are due to be put in place shortly) are intended to improve case management and reduce the need for adjournments in repossession cases. The authorities should continue to accelerate the court process for repossessions, and if necessary take further action to reduce NPLs, allocate losses and make progress to resolving the problem.

Although credit growth remains subdued, recent developments in residential and, especially, commercial property markets may be creating risks of another damaging property cycle. Property prices, especially in Dublin, have been rising rapidly albeit from low levels (Figure 6, Panels A-C). In this context, the recent macro-prudential measures (comprising caps on loan-to-value and loan-to-income ratios in residential property market lending) to build resilience among banks and borrowers and to reduce the chance of future credit and house price spirals, are welcome. It will be important that authorities monitor these measures closely to ensure they are effective. Furthermore, developments in the commercial property sector should be monitored on an ongoing basis and appropriate action taken if needed.

Regarding the housing market, the government should avoid subsidies for first-time home buyers, as these will be capitalised into prices, aggravating a potential price spiral and making it even harder for those with lower incomes to purchase homes. A more developed rental market would help moderate the property cycle, reduce household exposure to house price fluctuations, especially poorer ones that will be hardest hit if prices and rents continue to rise strongly. *Construction 2020* initiatives, including professionalised private rental markets, are thus welcome. Greater liberalisation of planning requirements including on building heights in Dublin would make supply more flexible to meet changing housing demand.

Easy monetary policy and search for yield by international investors has led to large increases in commercial property investment spending (Figure 6, Panel D) and rapid

Figure 6. **Property markets are reviving**

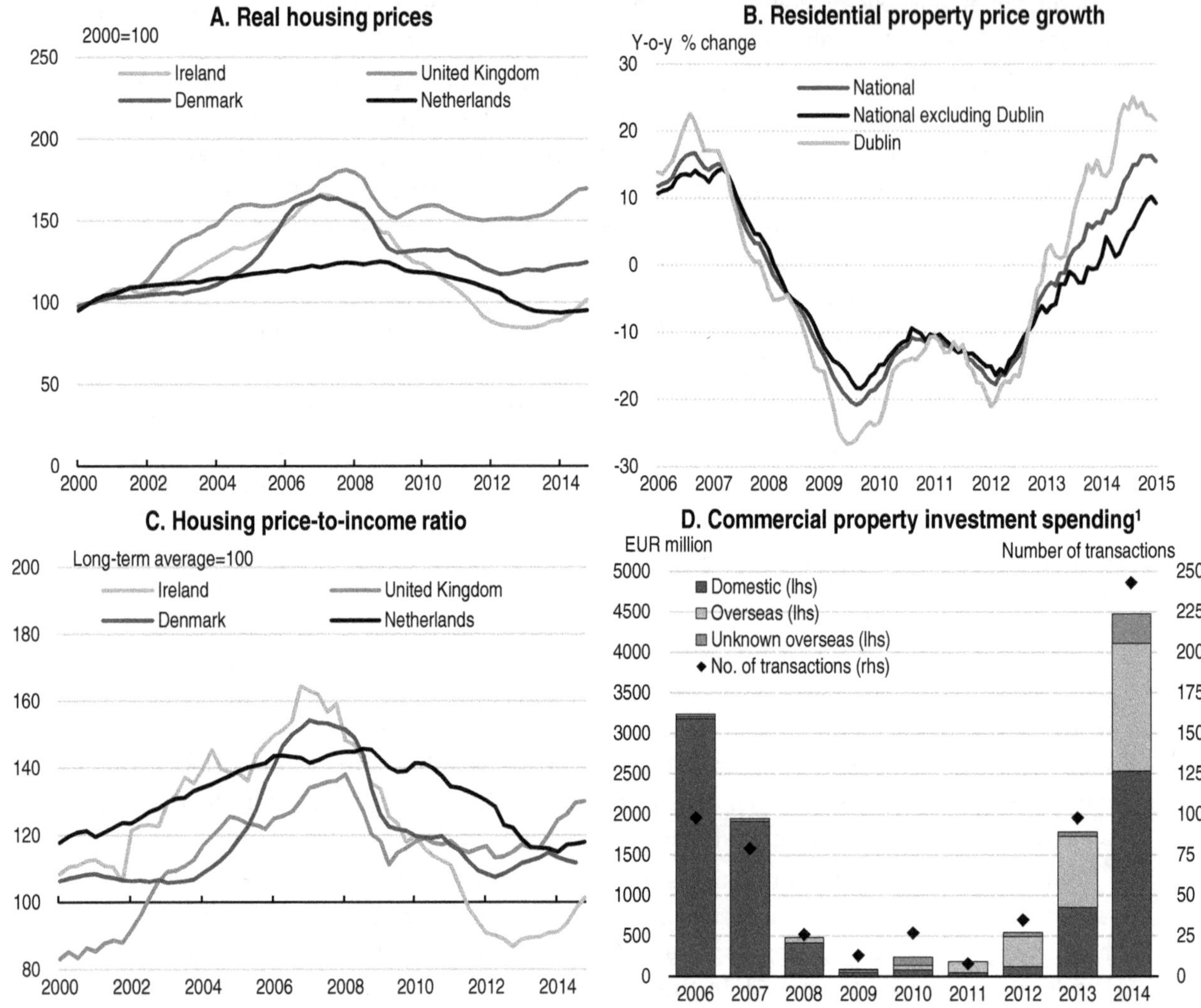

1. Investment spending refers to individual transactions worth at least EUR 1 million. All observations are for a 12 month period, except 2014 which refers to the first 9 months.

Source: Panels A and C: OECD, *OECD Economic Outlook Database*; Panel B: Central Statistics Office; Panel D: Central Bank of Ireland and CBRE Research.

StatLink http://dx.doi.org/10.1787/888933275071

growth rates of capital values in commercial properties and office rents (CBI, 2014). Moreover, a particularly high percentage of commercial real estate loans are already impaired. NAMA has also become a large player in many large commercial property development projects such as the Dublin Docklands Special Development Zone adopted in 2014, which raises its risk profile, making it critical that NAMAs operates in an arms-length commercial way, with strict government oversight of its activities to ensure it does so.

A variety of policies can help address the developing potential property market risks, as credit and housing cycles can reinforce each other. The credit register, which was recommended by the *2011 OECD Economic Survey*, is set to come into effect in 2016. The authorities should extend it to all types of lenders as quickly as possible to enhance its effectiveness In addition, macro-prudential policies can stabilise credit cycles as well as limit the probability and cost of systemic crises (Claessens, 2014; Jin et al., 2014). The role of macro-prudential policies are especially important for Ireland as it cannot use monetary policy to address the business cycle and the counter-cyclicality of fiscal policy is constrained by the need to reduce public debt. Furthermore, the post-crisis banking system, which is highly concentrated and includes three partly publicly-owned banks, creates the risk of "too big to fail" banks with potential fiscal implications.

The role of macro-prudential policies are especially important for Ireland as it cannot use monetary policy to address the business cycle and the counter-cyclicality of fiscal policy is constrained by high public debt. As recommended in the 2011 *OECD Survey of Ireland*, loan-to-value (LTV) and loan-to-income ratios came into effect in February 2015. The high levels of private debt (Figure 4; Table 3) and the recent history of the property market bubble suggest Ireland should make full use of all available macro-prudential tools. In this context, it is welcome that the authorities will operationalise counter-cyclical capital buffers (CCB) framework in Ireland from January 2016, as is required by the Capital Requirements Directive (CRD) IV. The central bank should also closely monitor the composition of bank lending so as to avoid concentration risk in particular asset classes.

Enhanced supervision of traditional financial institutions and instruments might be circumvented by new financial products resulting from technological changes as well as the engineering of products that, in a low interest environment, respond to the appetite for high yields by investors. In this environment, designing and implementing effective regulation, which balances financial stability, investors' protection and the opening of new financing channels for SMEs, represents a challenge for regulatory authorities (OECD, 2015).

In order to address investment financing constraints new sources of funding, including the Strategic Banking Corporation of Ireland (SBCI), (a wholesale lender to frontline SME lenders) and the Ireland Strategic Investment Fund (ISIF) have been established. By mid-2015, the SBCI had secured funding of EUR 800 million from the European Investment Bank, Germany's KfW and the National Pension Reserve Fund (now the ISIF). The ISIF has EUR 7.4 billion or around 4% of GDP from the former National Pension Reserve Fund with the dual mandate to invest on a commercial basis in a manner that supports economic activity and employment in Ireland. Both the SBCI and the ISIF should be monitored closely given the implied fiscal risks. The SBCI's operating model is to foster competition in the provision of credit rather than to compete directly with private operators. It is important to ensure that the SBCI and the ISIF do not crowd out private financing.

Making growth more inclusive

Looking across a broad range of indicators, Ireland delivers a high quality of life in many dimensions (Figure 7). Compared to the OECD average, the air is cleaner, more time is devoted to leisure, schools perform well for most students and the gender wage gap is smaller (Figure 8). Nonetheless, Ireland faces the challenge of having a very high share of its population being unemployed or inactive, and thus receiving no labour earnings. The unemployment rate among the poorly educated is significantly higher than the rate for those with tertiary education. This situation prevailed before the crisis, suggesting that it is a long-standing structural problem.

The Irish welfare system succeeds generally well in protecting the long-term unemployed and inactive from poverty, thus keeping income inequality near the OECD average. The transfer system is generous, as shown by Ireland providing the highest net replacement rate for long-term periods of unemployment (Figure 9). In addition to

Figure 7. **Wellbeing indicators are mixed**

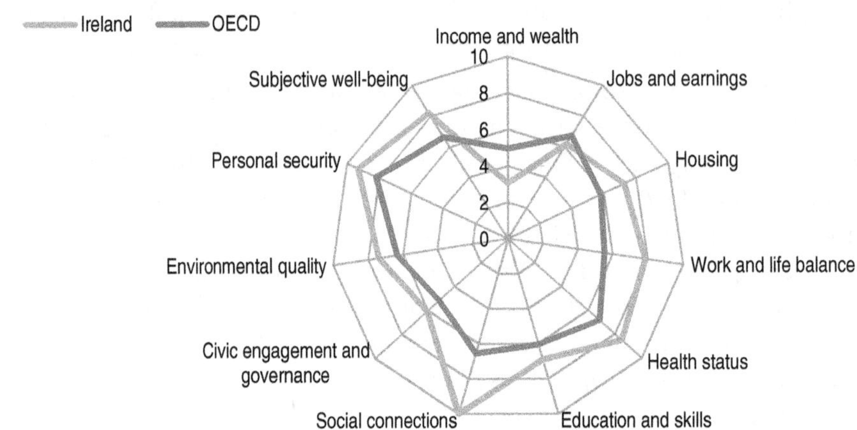

Note: Indicators are normalised to range between 10 (best) and 0 (worst) according to the following formula: (indicator value - minimum value) / (maximum value - minimum value) x 10.
Source: OECD, Better Life Index indicators 2015.

StatLink http://dx.doi.org/10.1787/888933275089

Figure 8. **Ireland performs well in some inclusiveness dimensions**[1]

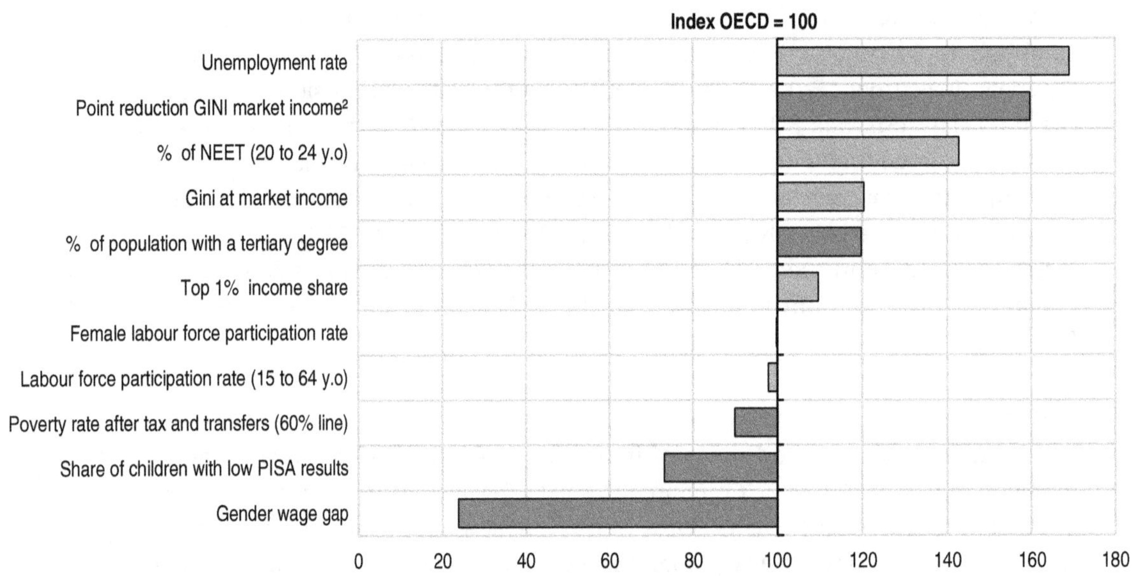

Notes: A green bar indicates that Ireland value is better than OECD average. A red bar indicates that Ireland value is worse than OECD average.
1. OECD average is for countries where data is available
2. And after taxes and transfers

Source: OECD various databases and the Paris School of Economics, *World Top Income Database*.

StatLink http://dx.doi.org/10.1787/888933275090

Figure 9. **Income support for the long-term unemployed is generous in Ireland**

Overall net replacement rates: net income while out of work in percentage of net income in work, 2011

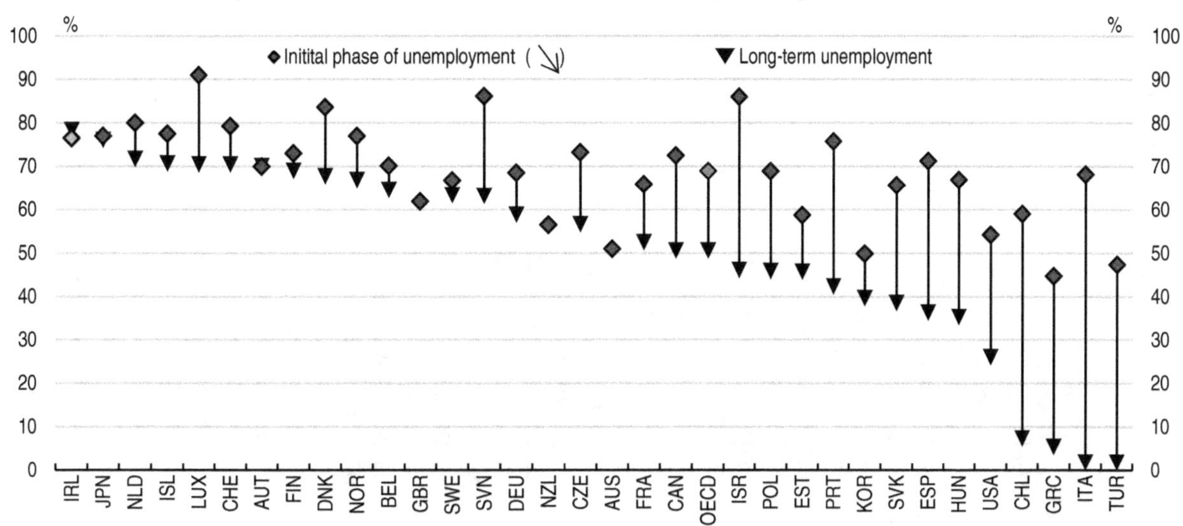

Source: OECD, *Tax-Benefit Models*, via *www.oecd.org/els/social/workincentives.*

StatLink http://dx.doi.org/10.1787/888933275100

allowances for jobseekers, Ireland provides a variety of welfare benefits related to housing, children and incentives to return to work. Active labour-market policies, which have been deeply reformed, play a key role in helping jobseekers return to work, including training.

Support to access affordable housing is an important policy to reduce poverty. A high percentage of low-income households benefits from subsidised rents in social housing or via rent supplement payments (OECD, 2014). Social housing accounts for about 8% of the total housing stock, with 70% of these units being occupied by families in the bottom two income quintiles. However, public investment in housing was cut dramatically in the wake of the crisis. At the same time, the rise in unemployment sharply lengthened the waiting list for social housing, although half of those on waiting lists receive government support via a rent supplement. The government has announced large increases in expenditure on social housing and rental subsidies (DECLG, 2014), which is appropriate.

In order to contain the fiscal cost of welfare programmes, Ireland targets them toward low-income households. A downside of this targeting, however, is that marginal effective tax rates - the combined effect on a person's earnings of income tax and the withdrawal of means-tested welfare benefits - can be very high (Figure 10). This reduces the financial incentives for the unemployed to seek re-employment. How these problems should be dealt with is a central issue to inclusive growth.

The cyclical recovery has been accompanied by robust employment gains and falling unemployment, but long-term unemployment has stayed very high (Figure 11). Many have been unemployed for more than 3 years and a significant share of families are headed by jobless parents. Getting more people back into work is the best way to spread the gains from the recovery, utilise people's potential talent and efficiently reduce income inequality. Some important policy levers for achieving this are: well-designed tax and welfare system; efficient activation policy; and better education and skills policies.

Figure 10. **Marginal effective tax rates are high for low income families**

67% of the average wage, single, two children, percent, 2014

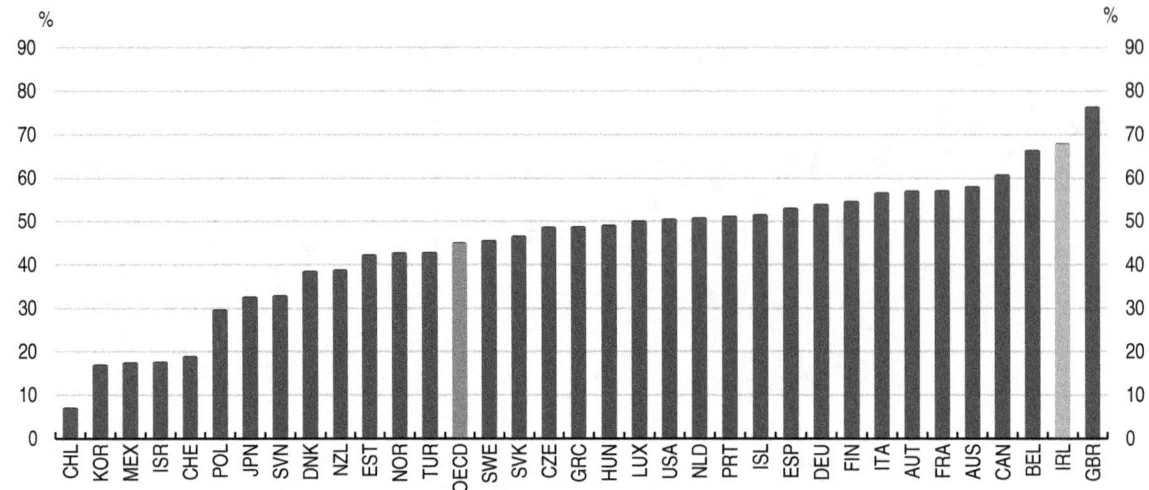

Source: OECD Taxing Wages (database).

StatLink http://dx.doi.org/10.1787/888933275119

Figure 11. **Long-term unemployment is high**

Share of unemployed, %

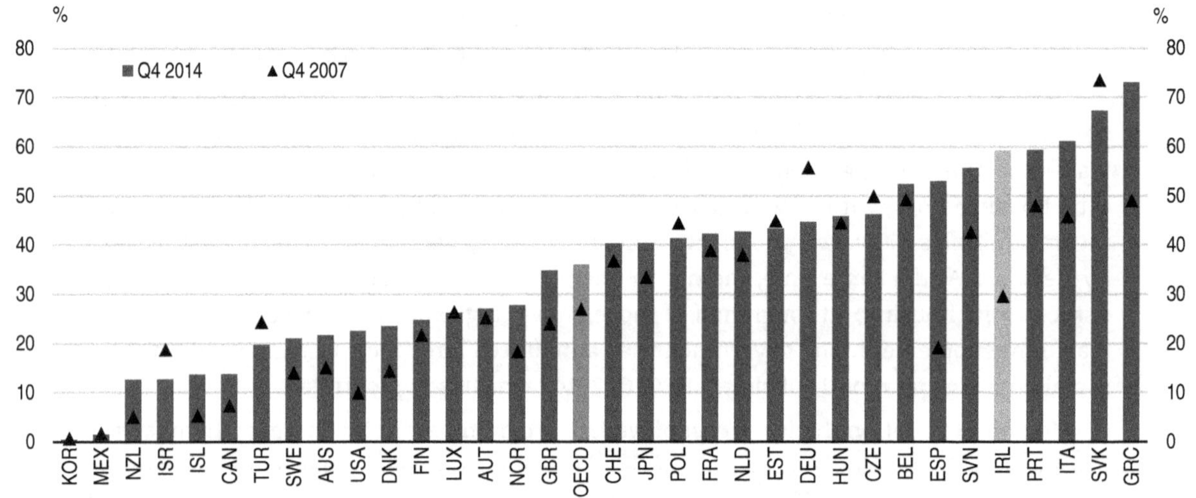

Note: Countries are shown in ascending order of the incidence of long-term unemployment in Q4 2014.

1. Data are not seasonally adjusted but smoothed using three-quarter moving averages. OECD is the weighted average of 33 OECD countries excluding Chile.
2. 2013 for Israel.

Source: OECD calculations based on quarterly national Labour Force Surveys (Cut-off date: 2 April 2015), *www.oecd.org/els/emp/onlineoecdemploymentdatabase.htm*.

StatLink http://dx.doi.org/10.1787/888933275128

Improving the tax and welfare system

Tax and welfare systems often create disincentives to work. High replacement rates discourage the decision to work (unemployment traps) and/or high marginal effective tax rates (METRs) discourage working more hours (low-income traps). Solving these problems involves unavoidable trade-offs between fiscal costs, work disincentive effects and social protection. As discussed above, Ireland combines high replacement rates for low-income individuals with a sharp reduction of welfare or in-work benefits and higher taxes as income rises, creating high effective replacement rates and strong disincentives for some households shifting from welfare to work.

There is evidence that unemployment traps exists in Ireland for some groups, and particularly those with a non-working partner and children. To improve work incentives without increasing poverty, the government has put in place an in-work payment, the Family Income Supplement (FIS), for lower-income working families with children, which partially compensate for the withdrawal of welfare upon return to work. However, as the FIS payment falls rapidly with income, those with low income face high marginal effective tax rates of over 60%. The government should reduce more gradually the FIS as income increases. Simulations undertaken by the Department of Finance with the ESRI Tax-benefit model show that, if combined with substantial increases in the FIS income limits, this would raise the disposable income of deciles 1 to 6, while also providing a greater incentive to work for the low-paid (O'Connor et al., 2015).

If the government were to reduce the FIS more gradually it would be important to bear in mind that its cost would have to be funded within the existing budgetary parameters. Preliminary estimates where the withdrawal rate is reduced from 60 to 32% and for a family with two children the income limit is increased from EUR 602 to 865 per week (other income limits rise by a similar ratio) suggest a cost of approximately EUR 200 million (0.1% of GDP) at current take-up rates of 33%. If the take-up rate increased to 100%, the reform would cost approximately EUR 700 million (0.4% of GDP).

In 2015, the government is also reforming the system of for housing benefits with a new Housing Assistance Payment that will depend on income whether from welfare or work, helping to reduce work disincentives. This is a welcome move and should be rolled out to all beneficiaries of payments to cover housing costs. This will reduce unemployment and low-income traps by removing the large spike in the marginal effective tax rate that occurred when someone crossed the threshold of 30 working hours per week when they lost their entire housing related benefits.

Efficient activation policy with strict implementation of conditionality

An important part of best practice active labour market policies is effectively implementing mutual obligations. This is also an efficient way to encouraging people to return to work while maintaining the generous transfer system. As the economy recovers and jobs availability increase job seeker obligations in return for the training and other support provided by the public employment services can be strictly enforced. In the 2000s, the sanction rate for refusal of active job search in Ireland was close to the lowest among OECD countries (OECD, 2013). McGuiness et al. (2011) show, with Irish data on unemployment benefit recipients, that those who do not actively commit to such activities, without effective control, encounter lower chances of entering employment.

Conditionality for unemployment benefits was tightened under "Pathways to Work" labour market reforms introduced in the early 2010s (OECD, 2013a). The percentage of beneficiaries penalised for non-compliance has increased since then. The sanction is applied gradually, beginning with a temporary reduction in benefits (around 25%) to a suspension up to 9 weeks. The sanction rate for those who failed to attend two initial interviews with the public employment service was 3.2% (of the inflow to the recipients) in 2014, which seems to be comparable with other OECD countries. The sanction for those who refuse to commit to active job search amounted to some 9200 cases, which is estimated to be around 3% of those who are registered as unemployed.

The conditionality approach can be even more enhanced in setting some objective criteria, as currently the sanction for non-compliance seems to be decided at the caseworker's discretion. For instance, the job seeker can be sanctioned when refusing a suitable job offer, against such criteria as wages, working hours, contract types, location, etc. However, it is not entirely clear how the job seeker is judged to have declined a "suitable" job offer. Some objective criteria would help to motivate the job seeker/recipient of benefits to accept a job, for example, defining the circumstances the job seeker has to accept a temporary contract, or defining the maximum reduction in wage relative to the previous job that can be considered as suitable.

The provision of social benefits (other than unemployment benefits) is currently not subject to conditionality in Ireland, even though many of beneficiaries could be considered fit for work. While such conditionality is not appropriate for all benefits, the authorities should consider the extent to which it could be extended.

Providing the right kinds of skills

Although much of the workforce is well qualified, many have insufficient skills to obtain sustainable employment. The OECD Survey of Adult Skills (PIAAC) signals that, despite improvements in recent years, adults in Ireland have lower skills than other OECD countries, especially regarding numeracy (Figure 12) and literacy skills. This relatively poor performance is partly explained by those aged 45-54 and 55-65, who also have relatively low levels of educational attainment. However, according to PIAAC, younger people in

Figure 12. **Numeracy skills are lacking**

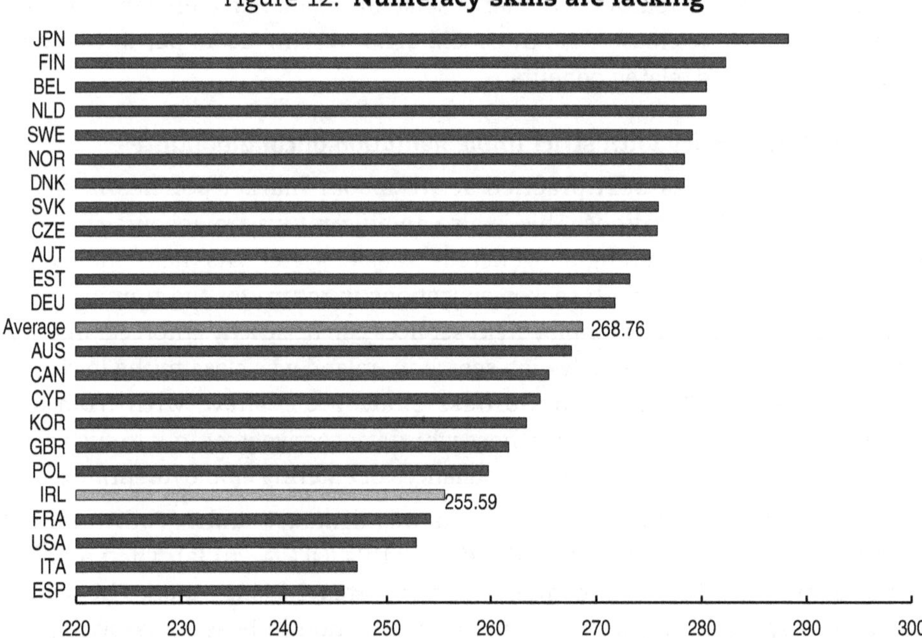

Note: Average numeracy score. Scores are on a 500 point scale and have been divided into 6 proficiency levels from below 1 through to 5. For example, someone with the average score in Ireland of 256 is level 2. This means that most of the time (67%) they can carry out a 2 or more step calculation involving whole numbers and percentages and interpret simple data in tables and charts.
Source: OECD Skills Outlook 2013.

StatLink http://dx.doi.org/10.1787/888933275134

Ireland also compare unfavourably with their peers in other OECD countries. To address these needs, SOLAS, the agency overseeing the delivery of training to the unemployed, launched its *Further Education and Training Strategy 2014-2019* to embed literacy and numeracy within further education and training provision. The Strategy has a literacy and numeracy plan for increasing participation of priority cohort groups such as older adults in literacy and numeracy programmes offered through the Education and Training Boards.

The situation for youth has improved but the unemployment rate and the rate of those not in employment, education or training remain above OECD and EU averages. Involuntary part-time employment is also high. The government informed by OECD advice (OECD, 2014a) developed a youth guarantee plan to transpose the EU Youth Guarantee to Ireland and implementing it should remain a priority.

There is also evidence of social inequalities in higher education participation. The social mix of students in school has a strong effect on educational outcomes (McCoy et al., 2014). The concentration of immigrant's in certain primary schools is increasing, with about 80% of children from immigrant backgrounds concentrated in 23% of schools. Providing disadvantaged schools with additional support, for example by attracting better teachers and providing additional tutoring, and avoiding excessive concentration of immigrants in disadvantaged schools would make Irish educational system more socially inclusive. Providing more information on educational options once they have left school, including vocational and technical options, would facilitate transitions to work. The government, in consultation with the youth work sector, should fine-tune the sector's learning programmes to further support youth transition through education and into work for students from as wide a set of backgrounds as possible.

The education and training system is also being reformed, including with new programmes aimed at providing skills relevant to the more knowledge-intensive economy that Ireland is becoming (e.g. *Momentum* and *Springboard*). Three-quarters of those who completed a *Springboard* course over the period 2011-2014 are no longer registered as unemployed. The apprenticeship system, narrowly geared towards the construction sector and hardly used at all by women, is also being reformed. Nevertheless, the pace of reform is very slow.

A new apprenticeship system is being developed. The Apprenticeship Council, established in November 2014, issued a call for new apprenticeship proposals, as recommended in previous *Economic Surveys* (e.g. OECD, 2013a). More progress has been made in the delivery of training to the unemployed. A Further Education and Training Services Plan was prepared by SOLAS in 2014, taking into account identified skills needs of employers. Some progress has been made in setting up the infrastructure to collect and link information on participants and outcomes. This information should be used to undertake timely statistical evaluation of training programmes. Based on that evaluation, resources should be reallocated to those schemes and providers that are effective in providing the skills needed to increase employability.

Better family policy: Encouraging voluntary participation of women

Low labour-market participation for women after the age of 30 and single parents can be explained by the high cost (Figure 13) and variable quality (Start Strong, 2014 and Hanafin, 2014) of childcare services. In the medium- to long- run, the family benefit system

Figure 13. **The cost of childcare is high**

Net cost (2012)

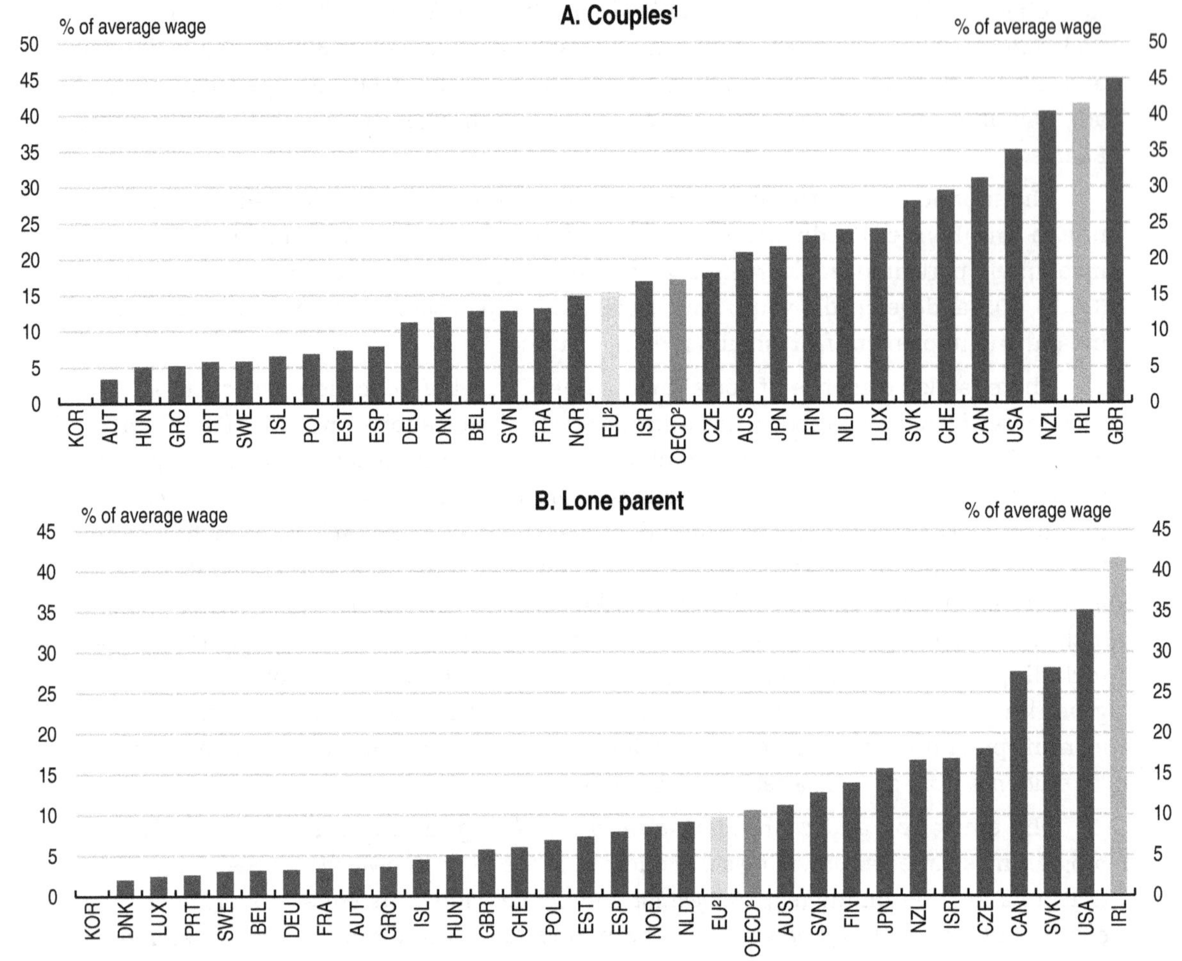

1. Couples where the first earner earns 100% of the average wage and the second earns 67% of the average wage. Lone parent earning 67% of the average wage. For Canada, the European Union, Finland, Norway, OECD, Slovak Republic, Slovenia and the United Kingdom, childcare benefits refer to childcare and other benefits.
2. EU and OECD averages exclude Chile, Italy, Mexico and Turkey.

Source: OECD, *Tax-Benefit Models*; *www.oecd.org/els/social/workincentives*.

StatLink http://dx.doi.org/10.1787/888933275145

should be revamped so that spending on cash benefits and childcare services are more balanced. In Ireland cash benefits and childcare services account for 3% and 1% of GDP respectively versus 1.3% and 1% of GDP on average in the OECD. Such a spending neutral reform would both encourage more female labour force participation and, in some case, correct distortions to incentives to supply labour (see above).

Fostering productivity

The Irish economy has many structural features that have facilitated the development of a vibrant business sector and attracted a high level of foreign investment, even in the aftermath of the crisis. These include it being English speaking and in the EU, its skilled workforce, a capacity to attract skilled migrants (Chapter 2), low corporate taxes, flexible labour and product market regulations, the capacity of Ireland's universities to generate the talent firms need, a highly effective foreign investment support agency, and a pragmatic and responsive public administration.

Productivity growth, however, has been falling for some time, reflecting both cyclical and structural factors (Figure 14). The boom resulted in a misallocation of resources, contributing to a decline in productivity. The slowdown in trend growth may also be related to a recent slowdown of investment in knowledge-based capital (a broad investment in knowledge including computerised information, innovative intellectual property (e.g. patents) and economic competencies, such as organisational capabilities) (Figure 15).

Figure 14. **Ireland's trend GDP growth rate has declined**

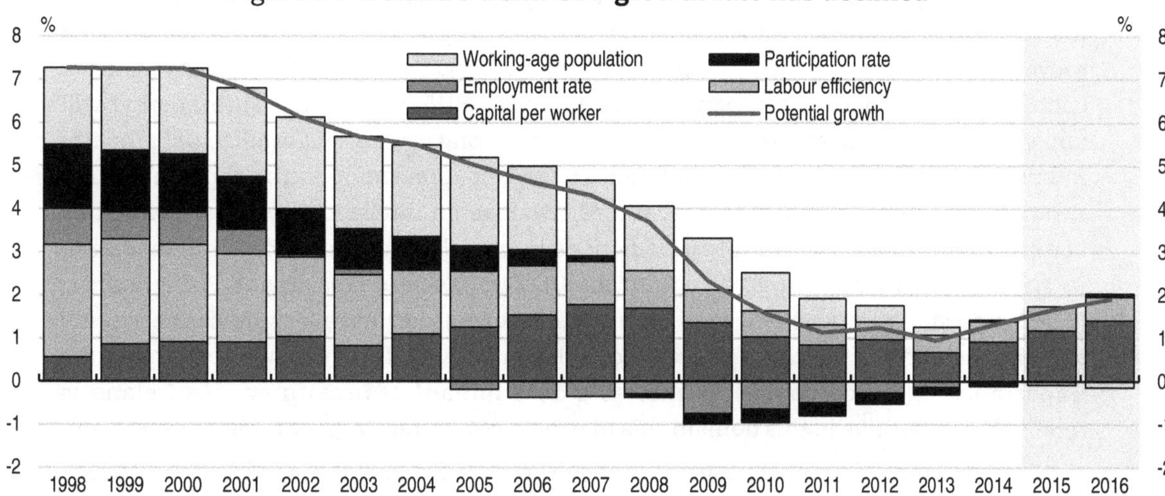

Source: *OECD Economic Outlook, Long-Term Database.*

StatLink http://dx.doi.org/10.1787/888933275152

Figure 15. **Investment in Knowledge Based Capital has slowed**

Investment in KBC, annual average growth

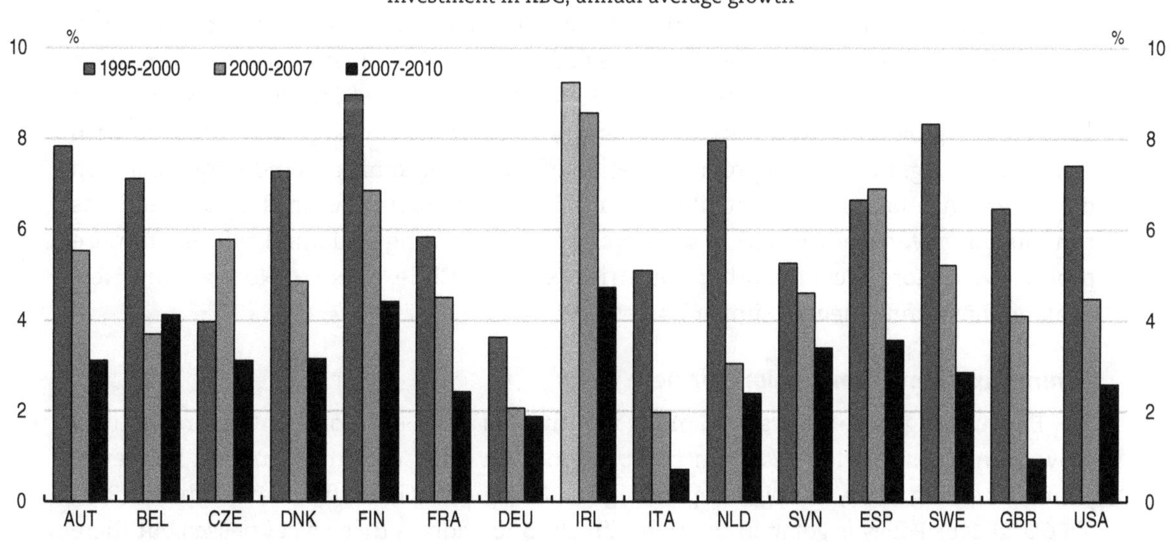

Source: Corrado et al. (2014).

StatLink http://dx.doi.org/10.1787/888933275168

Maintaining FDI attractiveness

Foreign investment has been the source of whole new sectors, such as medical devices, and contributes significantly to jobs, innovation and exports. The foreign investment support agency, IDA Ireland, should continue to target key foreign firms, as the presence of one multinational tends to attract others (Barry, et al., 2003; Worrall, 2014). To ensure better linkages of multinationals to the wider economy, the government should continue to support business accelerators and incubators, which have a proven record of fostering a company start-up environment in the IT sector (Connolly, 2014).

A low and stable corporate tax rate is also important for attracting investment. Increasingly significant in the context of growing general concern about tax avoidance by multinationals worldwide is the reputation of the Irish system as fair and transparent. The move to abolish the so-called "double Irish" from 2020 is welcome- the legislative change came into effect for new companies from 1 January 2015, while a transition period will apply until 2020 for existing companies. Given the strong presence of intellectual property intensive IT and pharmaceutical companies in Ireland, preventing artificial profit shifting through the payment of non-market-priced royalties on intellectual property owned by companies in zero or low tax rate jurisdictions is crucial. Ireland should continue to keep its transfer pricing rules up to date with the OECD/G20's Base Erosion and Profit Shifting (BEPS) project. Although changes to tax rules elsewhere may have a significant economy wide impact (Box 1), the closing of tax loopholes in other countries may also increase the importance of the corporate tax rate as a determinant of investment. As Ireland is relatively competitive in this domain this may help it to attract greater foreign investment.

Maintaining a favourable regulatory environment for business is also important to help foster a return to higher productivity growth, especially amongst home-grown firms, whose performance lags significantly behind the foreign owned sector (Haugh, 2013). For this purpose, Ireland needs to maintain a strong focus on policies to raise productivity. One option is an independent agency that would pull together on a whole-of-government basis the many of strands of policy needed to raise productivity. For example, this could be achieved by expanding the role of the National Competitiveness Council to deal with productivity in the broad sense. The renewed Council should continue to maintain a permanent research staff of sufficient size to fulfil a mandate of identifying obstacles to productivity growth, advocating the necessary reforms, and engage in a dialogue with stakeholders regarding the appropriate design of micro-economic and industry regulation measures. The Australia Productivity Commission was a forerunner in this area, and has compiled a proven track record of developing and advocating structural reforms to raise productivity. More recently, other countries (such as Chile, Mexico, Norway and New Zealand) have implemented similar bodies.

Tuning-up innovation support for new firms

Encouraging more innovation among new firms is a key lever for boosting productivity growth and jobs (Lawless, 2013) In comparison with other countries, Ireland has fewer young patenting firms, less public spending on R&D, and less industry financed public R&D (OECD, 2014b). Policy is going in the right direction to address these weaknesses but there is scope for improvement.

Ireland's total public support to business R&D is not especially high in relation to its GDP and is skewed towards R&D tax credits. R&D tax credits have the advantage that they avoid the "picking winners" problem associated with direct grants. They also should require fewer administrative resources to operate than direct grants. However, R&D tax incentives can protect incumbents to the detriment of new entrants (Bravo-Biosca et al., 2013). Direct support makes SMEs more likely to carry out R&D (Czarnitski and Ebersberger, 2010). Even if R&D tax incentives contain carry-over provisions and refunds as in Ireland, young firms may not fully benefit from the schemes if they lack the upfront funds to start an innovative project, and in these cases public funding may be more beneficial (Busom et al., 2014).Given that both types of support have advantages, a more balanced mix should be used and the mix of support should be shifted towards direct grants.

Young firms and SMEs would also benefit from research networks due to their limited in-house R&D resources, but they engage in less collaboration because they lack absorptive capacity. Research staff and student placements can play a role in lifting absorptive capacity. The steady expansion of employment based research programme for graduate students should continue. Increasing absorptive capacity also requires improving smaller firm management knowledge of open innovation networks, which could be facilitated by expanding Enterprise Ireland's mentoring programmes to include a component on innovation collaboration, intellectual property protection as well as international sales.

Effective collaboration also requires tuning public research institutes so they can better meet smaller firm needs. Young firms and SMEs have fewer resources and therefore need faster direct pay-offs from innovation (Mina et al., 2008) and projects that focus on improving product quality and production processes (Novero, 2008). Enterprise Ireland should ensure its new Technology Centres are demand driven, and that they encompass consulting, research, technology advisory and testing (Mina et al., 2009). The total budget of the 15 centres under development is only one third of that of the budget of Ireland's successful agri-food Research Technology Organisation, Teagasc (DJEI, 2014). The large stock of foreign investment in Ireland could be further leveraged by introducing a procurement database/market where large firms place orders for services or products that smaller firms could bid to produce.

Constraints on finance can be a major obstacle for new, innovative firms. The provision of venture capital in Ireland is above the EU average. The government has introduced a variety of new tools to address financing needs of firms not suited for traditional bank lending (OECD, 2013a). It will be important to maintain private sector involvement in these arrangements and monitor the performance of the various venture capital funds.

Getting more from competition

Increasing competition reduces monopoly rents, which are a source of income inequality, inefficiency and less inclusive growth. In a welcome move, the government overhauled the Competition Law Framework in 2014. The Competition Authority and the National Consumer Agency were merged into the Competition and Consumer Protection Commission (CCPC) and the CCPC has been given new powers.

There is room to intensify competition in Ireland in less trade exposed sectors. Ireland is ranked worst in the OECD for restrictive regulation on forms of legal professional cooperation in the OECD's PMR Index. The Legal Services Bill 2011 meets many of the CCPC's recommendations to enhance competition in the legal sector. The government should also introduce a separate conveyancing profession, which has lowered the cost of these services in the United Kingdom (OECD, 2013a).

The Government partly implemented the CCPC's recommendations to increase competition in the port sector by issuing some new self-handling cargo licences. However, general cargo handling licences have an automatic renewal clause, protecting incumbents. The state-owned port companies should require a tender or other competitive process for renewal of licences.

In the electricity sector, the transmission grid is independently operated by Eirgrid, but is owned by the incumbent generator, the Electricity Supply Board (ESB). The government should work towards the fuller separation of transmission and generation activities so as enhance competition in the sector. In addition, generation remains concentrated and competition should be further enhanced by the sale of some of ESB's current capacity.

Migration contributes to reducing skill mismatches

Migration plays an important role in the Irish labour market. The economic crisis triggered a rapid increase in emigration, in large part among highly-skilled and people in employment. More recent data shows that while total emigration has started to decline, emigration by individuals with tertiary education continues to increase. Despite the general improvement in the Irish economy and its labour market, the outflow of university graduates exceeds the inflow. Productivity prospects of domestic companies, whose ability to hire workers abroad is limited, are more likely to be affected by this net outflow of qualified workers than multinationals, which are more successful in international recruitment. This risks that the already large productivity gap between domestic firms and multinationals will widen further; it also highlights the need for Ireland to optimise policies to retain and attract qualified workers, and to facilitate that all companies can take full advantage of these policies.

A high proportion of immigrants are also highly-skilled. This pattern of "brains exchange" reduces skill mismatches but also raises the challenge of integrating immigrants. As the economy recovers, the gap between immigrants and Irish workers in terms of employment probabilities is receding to pre-crisis levels (González Pandiella et al., 2015). Ireland is also starting to experience challenges associated with the integration of second generation immigrants. In that respect, providing students of foreign language background English language training is crucial.

Ireland will continue to need skilled immigrants. That challenge will become more acute, as wages in traditional source countries catch up (Westmore, 2014) and more countries join the global competition for skills. Ireland has responded by more regular (bi-annual) evidence-based reviews of occupations eligible for the Critical Skills Employment Permit. Ireland has also made good progress in reducing processing times for employment permits, from 36 days in January 2013 to 23 days in April 2015. This is among the lower processing times in the OECD (OECD, 2014c). Given the importance of migration to Ireland it should continue to optimise its migration selection system by making further use of IT in employment permits processes.

Ireland has introduced self-declaration and the *Trusted Partner Initiative*, whereby the submission of documentation is replaced by a declaration by the employer that the requisites are met. The *Initiative* will reduce administration significantly. Ireland should encourage and fine tune such schemes and monitor the system to make sure it works for SMEs.

Better use could be made of international students as a channel for high-skill immigration. After graduation the job-search period allowed in Ireland ranges from six to twelve months. Countries with a higher share of international students allow for longer job-search periods, (OECD, 2014c). It can reach up to 30 months in Australia. Another avenue to make Ireland more attractive is post-study employment permits. Exempting international students from the employment permit fee in highly demanded areas where there are significant skills shortages in Ireland (provided they meet the criteria for obtaining the permit) would contribute to smoothing the transition to work.

Improving environmental sustainability

Ensuring an environmental sustainable pattern of growth is also a critical part of improving well-being in the medium-term. Clean water and air, less waste and its efficient disposal and uncongested cities are key elements of high standards of living and better quality of life. Fostering clean technologies, products and services by the business sector can help make Ireland more resilient to volatility in the price of fossil fuels. Developing green technologies, especially in areas of comparative advantage such as agriculture, can contribute to higher productivity growth and employment opportunities at a variety of skill levels in rural areas.

The Irish Environmental Protection Agency (EPA) estimates that without new initiatives Ireland's greenhouse gas emissions will exceed its EU mandated target for non-ETS (Emission Trading System) emissions for the period 2013-2020 (Table 4; EPA, 2015). The government is developing new energy and low-carbon initiative policies as part of the development of a National Climate Change Mitigation Plan and the establishment of cross-sectoral coordination processes and commitments through the soon-to-be-enacted Climate Action and Low Carbon Development Bill 2015. Achieving sustainability goals will

Table 4. **Climate change scorecard**

Greenhouse gas emissions, thousands tons of carbon dioxide (CO_2) equivalent[1]

	Year	Actual	Target
Total greenhouse gas emissions	1990	55 246	...
	2000	68 216	...
	2008-12	308 509	314 200
	2020	..	Single EU-wide cap of 20% below 1990 emissions
Emissions Trading System (ETS)	2008-12		
	2013-20	...	Single EU-wide cap of 21% below 2005 emissions
Non-ETS greenhouse gas emissions	2008-12	219 000	
	2020	...	Reduce emissions 20% below 2005 emissions
Non-ETS EU annual emissions allocation (AEA) target	2020		37 500
Renewable electricity (% of total electricity generation)	1990		
	2002	7%	
	2013	21%	
	2020	...	
Area with greatest potential to reduce emissions			Agriculture, buildings and transport

1. Excluding land-use, land-use change and forestry (LULUCF).

Source: OECD (2014), "Greenhouse gas emissions", *OECD Environment Statistics* (database); EC (2014), *Technical Paper: Kyoto Ambition Mechanism Report*, 30 April 2014 OECD (2015), *OECD Electricity and Heat Generation* (database); Irish Environmental Protection Agency (EPA), (2013) *Ireland's Greenhouse Gas Emission Projections 2012-2030*.

necessarily involve public support, but it is important that realisation of these goals is supported and promoted on the basis of least cost interventions, and market-based tools. A promising low-cost route is to step up programmes to improve energy efficiency of housing (Ameli et al., 2015), which can help not only reduce GHG emissions but also improve health and equity outcomes.

Urban sprawl is a problem, especially in Dublin. It creates air pollution and congestion, which are becoming apparent again with the return to robust economic growth. Sustainable urban and housing planning, now focused on increasing density of the metropolitan area, will help to increase the viability of public transport that can not only help reduce emissions but also increase the welfare of all citizens, especially those on lower-incomes. A return to healthier public finances should facilitate greater public investment in public transport, infrastructure and services, which was heavily cut during the crisis. However, projects should be evaluated on an ex-ante basis. The coverage of the public transport network and the extent of bike lanes are below European city averages (EIU, 2009). A priority for public capital spending, and complementary to the government's expansion of social housing policy, should be increasing urban public transport, especially to more deprived parts of the metropolitan area. The Dublin bike scheme has been significantly expanded since 2009 and cycling trips into Dublin City have doubled since 2006. Further dedicated cycling lanes and expansion of the Dublin bike scheme would also help to cheaply reduce carbon emissions as well as improve labour market access and social inclusion of those on lower incomes.

Water stress is among the lowest in the OECD, but in some areas household water quality is an issue due to under-investment (EPA, 2015a) and dairy sector expansion poses new challenges. In a welcome move the government introduced household water charges, which are still among the lowest in the OECD. This new funding mechanism has been introduced in tandem with significant reforms of the water sector in Ireland, to improve the overall governance from a Water Framework Directive implementation perspective, and to bring a greater strategic approach and increased efficiency to investment through the establishment of a national public water utility, Irish Water. The introduction of household water charges should be accompanied by a well-communicated programme of infrastructure renewal. This can help to improve public acceptance of the charges and Irish Water's programme to fix leaks is promising in this regard. The expansion of dairying following the removal of EU quotas should be accompanied by more innovation to mitigate negative air and water quality side-effects. Although slowly improving, the development of environmental technologies appears to be modest by OECD standards. One avenue to boost this quickly would be to target foreign investment by an "anchor" multinational leader in dairy related environmental technologies, coupled with greater funding to the public research organisation, Teagasc, from a levy on the dairy industry.

Household waste per capita has been one of the highest in the OECD but new policies are now reducing it. Landfill levy charges have been increased significantly to discourage landfill use, which is now declining: for the first time, the amount of waste recycled nationally in 2014 exceeded the total waste landfilled. A new "3-bin" household waste separation system is being progressively introduced and from July 2016 households will pay by weight for waste, thereby incentivising further reduction in waste generation. In addition, a new thermal waste treatment plant is due to come on stream in 2017. These efforts could be complemented with greater incentives for firms via taxation and direct support to innovate to reduce the amount of packaging material and increase the recyclability of packaging material.

Bibliography

Ameli, N. and N. Brandt (2015), "What Impedes Household Investment in Energy Efficiency and Renewable Energy?", *OECD Economics Department Working Papers*, No. 1222, OECD Publishing, Paris, *http://dx.doi.org/10.1787/5js1j15g2f8n-en*.

Barry, F., H. Goerg and E. Strobl (2003), "Foreign Direct Investment, Agglomerations and Demonstration Effects: An Empirical Investigation", *Weltwirtschaftliches Archiv*, Vol. 139, pp. 583-600.

Bravo Biosca, A., C. Criscuolo and C. Menon (2013),"What Drives the Dynamics of Business Growth?", *OECD Science, Technology and Industry Policy Papers*, No. 1.

Busom, I., B. Corchuelo and E. Martínez-Ros (2014,) "Tax Incentives… or Subsidies for Business R&D?, *Small Business Economics*, Vol. 43, pp. 571-596.

Causa, O. and Å. Johansson (2010), "Intergenerational Social Mobility in OECD Countries", *OECD Journal: Economic Studies*, Vol. 2010/1, *http://dx.doi.org/10.1787/eco_studies-2010-5km33scz5rjj*.

Central Bank of Ireland (2014), *Macrofinancial Review*, Volume 2, Dublin.

Central Bank of Ireland (2015), *Macrofinancial Review*, Volume 1, Dublin.

Claessens, S. (2014), "An Overview of Macroprudential Policy Tools", *IMF Working Papers*, No. 214.

Connolly, P. (2014), "A Tech Ecosystem Develops in Silicon Docks: The Rise of Dublin as a *Global tech Hub*", Pamela Newenham (ed.) Liberties Press, Dublin.

Corrado, C., J. Haskel, C. Jona-Lasinio and M. Iommi (2014), "Internationally comparable macro-estimates of investment in intangible assets at the industry level: INTAN – Invest" available at *www.INTAN-Invest.net*.

Czarnitsk, D. and J. Macintosh (2006), "Crowding and Private Equity: Canadian Evidence", Journal of Business Venturing, Vol. 21 (5), pp569-609, September.

Department of Environment, Community and Local Government (DECLG) (2014), *Support, Supply and Reform*, November 2014.

Department of Justice and Equality (2014), *Report of the Expert Group on Repossessions*, Dublin.

Department of Jobs, Enterprise and Innovation (DJEI) (2014), *State Investment in Research and Development 2013-2014*.

Department of Taoiseach (2014), *Draft National Risk Assessment*.

Economist Intelligence Unit (EIU) (2009), *European Green City Index*, available at: *www.siemens.com/press/pool/de/events/corporate/2009-12-Cop15/European_Green_City_Index.pdf*.

Environment Protection Agency (EPA) (2015), *Ireland's Greenhouse Gas Emission Projections 2014-2035*.

Environment Protection Agency (EPA) (2015a), *Drinking Water Report 2013*.

Fitzgerald, J. (2013), "The Effect of Redomiciled Plcs on GNP and the Irish Balance of Payments, *ESRI Quarterly Economic Commentary*, Spring 2013.

Hanafin, S. (2014), "Report on the Quality of Pre-school Services: Analysis of Pre-school Inspection Reports", Dublin: Tusla, Child and Family Agency.

Irish Fiscal Advisory Council (IFAC) (2015), *Fiscal Assessment Report, June 2015*.

Jin, Y., P. Lenain and P. O'Brien (2014), "Macroprudential Policy Tools in Norway: Strengthening Financial System Resilience", *OECD Economics Department Working Papers*, No. 1126, OECD Publishing, *http://dx.doi.org/10.1787/5jz2mm2vbhjk-en*.

Johansson, Å. et al. (2008), "Taxation and Economic Growth", *OECD Economics Department Working Papers*, No. 620, OECD Publishing, *http://dx.doi.org/10.1787/241216205486*.

Kelly, E., S. McGuinness, P. O'Connell, A. González Pandiella, and D. Haugh (2015), "How Well Does Ireland Integrate Migrants into its Labour Market?", *OECD Economics Department Working Papers*, forthcoming.

Kennedy, S., Y. Jin and D. Haugh (2015), "Taxes, Income and Economic Mobility in Ireland: New Evidence from Tax Records Data", *OECD Economics Department Working Papers*, forthcoming.

Lawless, M. (2013), "Age or Size? Contribution to Job Creation", *Central Bank of Ireland Research Technical Paper*, 2/RT/13.

McCoy, S., E. Smyth, D. Watson and M. Darmody (2014), "Leaving School in Ireland: A Longitudinal Study of Post School Transitions", *ESRI Research Series*, No. 36.

McGuiness. S, P.J O'Connell, E. Kelly (2011), "Carrots without Sticks: The Impact of Job Search Assistance in a Regime with Minimal Monitoring and Sanctions", WP 409, Economic and Social Research Institute (ESRI), Ireland.

Mina. A, D. Connell and A. Hughes, "Models of Technology Development in Intermediate Research Organisations", Centre for Business Research, University of Cambridge, Working paper No. 396.

Motohashi, K. (2008), "Growing R&D Collaboration of Japanese Firms and Policy Implications for Reforming the National Innovation System", *Asia Pacific Business Review*, 14:3, pp. 339-361.

Novero, S. (2008), "Public Interventions Supporting Innovation in Small and Medium-Size Firms. Successes or Failures? A Probit Analysis", *Ceris-CNr Working Paper*, No. 11.

O'Brien, D. and J. Scally (2012), "Cost Competitiveness and Export Performance of the Irish Economy", *Quarterly Bulletin, Central Bank of Ireland*, 3 July.

O'Connor, B., T. Hynes, D. Haugh and P. Lenain (2015), "The Distributional Consequences of Growth and Employment Enhancing Tax and Welfare Changes in Ireland", *OECD Economics Department Working Papers*, forthcoming.

OECD (2011), *OECD Report on Experiences with Structural Separation*, OECD Publishing, Paris

OECD, (2013), *Employment Outlook*, OECD Publishing, Paris.

OECD (2013a), *OECD Economic Survey of Ireland*, OECD Publishing, Paris, *http://dx.doi.org/10.1787/eco_surveys-irl-2013-en.*

OECD (2014), "Policies to Promote Access to Good-Quality Affordable Housing, Working Party on Social Policy", *DELSA/WP1(2014)1.*

OECD (2014a), *OECD Youth Action Plan: Options for an Irish Youth Guarantee*, January 2014, OECD Publishing.

OECD (2014b), *OECD Science, Technology and Industry Outlook 2014*, OECD Publishing, Paris, *http://dx.doi.org/10.1787/sti_outlook-2014-en.*

OECD (2014c), *International Migration Outlook 2014*, OECD Publishing, *http://dx.doi.org/10.1787/sti_outlook-2014-en.*

OECD (2015), *New Approaches to SME and Entrepreneurship Financing: Broadening the Range of Instruments*, OECD Publishing.

O'Farrell, R. (2015), "Have Wage Developments Improved Ireland's International Competitiveness since 2008?", *The Economic and Social Review*, Vol. 43, No. ??.

Start Strong (2014), "Childcare: Business or Profession?", available at *www.startstrong.ie/files/Childcare_Business_or_Profession_Full_Report_Web_Version.pdf.*

Westmore, B. (2014), "International Migration: the Relationship with Economic and Policy Factors in the Home and Destination country", *OECD Economics Department Papers*, No. 1140, OECD Publishing, *http://dx.doi.org/10.1787/5jz123h8nd7l-en.*

Worrall, J.J., "Game Change: Google Moves to the Docks", in Silicon Docks: The Rise of Dublin as a *Global Tech Hub*, Pamela Newenham (ed.), Liberties Press, Dublin.

© OECD 2015

Annex

Structural reform

The objective of this Annex is to review action taken since the previous Survey (October 2013) on the main recommendations from previous Surveys, which are not reviewed and assessed in the current Survey.

Rebalancing the economy

Recommendations from previous *Survey*	Action taken since the October 2013 *Survey*
To retain access to financial markets under sustainable and affordable terms, further reduce the public debt-to-GDP ratio. If growth projections are not met and if financial markets conditions are appropriate, the automatic stabilisers should be allowed to operate around the structural consolidation path.	Fiscal policy, strong economic growth and positive stock-flow adjustments have contributed to reducing the public debt-to-GDP ratio. It is projected to decline from 123% in 2013 to 105% of GDP at end 2015, according to the national authorities.
Fully implement the strategy to reduce non-performing loans taking account of the steps taken to date, so as to sustain on-going balance sheet adjustments, improve bank health and foster the gradual recovery of domestic demand.	NPLs are reducing as banks' implement restructuring strategies. These include a re-underwriting of new but reduced exposures to challenged customers, deleveraging, and pursuing legal options to generate recoveries in cases where no other solution is viable. The Mortgage Arrears Resolution Process, in place since 2011, was strengthened to accelerate debt restructuring: performance targets for borrowers in arrears over 90 days for main mortgage lenders were introduced. In April 2015, new rules replacing quarterly targets with new requirements to conclude sustainable solutions for a majority of distressed loans by the end of 2015 came into effect. The Central Bank has written to banks setting out new requirements that concluded sustainable solutions are in place for most distressed borrowers by the end of 2015 (the Mortgage Arrears Resolution Targets process).
After exit from the current EU-IMF programme, consider international backstop options to provide support in the event of an unexpected shock.	Following exit from the programme, Ireland returned successfully to the long-term bond markets, without a pre-arranged precautionary credit facility. Ireland's bond yields are trading at historically low levels. Ireland also completed early repayment of 81% of its IMF programme loans in March 2015.

Reinvigorating growth

Recommendations from previous *Survey*	Action taken since the October 2013 *Survey*
While Ireland is generally business friendly, there is a need to prioritise further structural reforms. To ease doing business, increase competition in legal services and reduce licence and permit fees and waiting times.	The Legal Services Regulation Bill is under discussion in Parliament. The Bill aims to operationalise the new Legal Services Regulatory Authority without delay in 2015.
Continue to emphasise fiscal measures that minimise harm to growth and equity, such as the residential property tax. Review existing tax and welfare structures to address better labour force participation of low-wage workers.	In the 2015 Budget; income tax was reduced (the threshold at which income tax is due was raised and the higher rate of income tax was reduced from 41% to 40%); the Universal Social Charge, income tax-like social security contribution, was also reduced. The Back To Work Family Dividend was introduced. The benefit aims to help families to move from social welfare into employment: people with qualified children, taking up employment and becoming no longer eligible to certain benefits, obtain a weekly payment for up to 2 years.
Address long-term spending pressures in the pension system. Place environmental protection more at the centre of the tax, charges and subsidy policy choices.	The pensionable age was increased to 66 in State Pension (Contributory) in January 2014. The payment to 65-66 years olds was abolished in State Pension (Transition) in January 2014. A new Single Public Service Pension Scheme has been in place since January 2013: in the scheme, benefits are based on career average earnings, not final salary. The Finance Act 2014 lists natural gas and biogas as transport fuels and sets the rate of excise at the EU minimum rate for a period of 8 years.

Recommendations from previous *Survey*	Action taken since the October 2013 *Survey*
To improve public trust in Government, increase transparency and accountability of Government institutions.	The Freedom of Information (FOI) Act 2014 extends FOI to almost all public bodies. The Open Data Initiative makes data held by public bodies available and easily accessible online for reuse and redistribution. Ireland became a full member of the Open Government Partnership in July 2014. The Houses of the Oireachtas (Inquiries, Privileges and Procedures) Act 2013 introduced a comprehensive legislative framework for parliamentary inquiries. A comprehensive review on accountability of the Civil Service was conducted, including through public consultation. The review's recommendations are being implemented. The Government introduced a new system for State Board Appointments in 2014.

Labour market activation policies

Recommendations from previous *Survey*	Action taken since the October 2013 *Survey*
To avoid rising structural unemployment and a drift into social exclusion, prioritise engagement with the long-term unemployed and increase the number of caseworkers supporting them, through internal redeployment.	The long-term unemployed have been increasingly involved in activation policies, which will be put on a more systematic footing with the launch of JobPath in mid-2015.
To reduce mismatches between supply and demand of skills, better align the content of education and training schemes so that they provide skills required in the expanding sectors.	SOLAS, the agency overseeing the delivery of further education and training to the unemployed, published the first annual Further Education and Training Service Plan in 2014. The Expert Group on Future Skills Needs (EGFSN) and the Strategic Labour Market Research Unit identify such required skills. The Higher Education Authority performance compacts with Higher Education Institutions 2014-2016 require them to report on how they are responding to labour market needs including the recommendations of EGFSN. The ICT Skills Action Plan 2014-2018 was launched aimed at addressing the 44 000 job openings expected to arise over that period for ICT graduates across all sectors of the economy.
Focus limited fiscal resources on policies empirically-proven to improve employability; this will require systematic evaluation of labour-market programmes through consistent tracking and randomised trials, followed by decisions to close down ineffective schemes while strengthening successful ones.	Some evidence on effectiveness has been found for the Momentum programme (vocational training for the long-term unemployed); the TUS programme (community work placement scheme to which referral was based on random assignment from among the long-term unemployed); and the JobBridge internship programme. Resources have been increased in internships and training.
To minimise the detrimental and enduring impact of long-term unemployment, establish a youth compact whereby those in unemployment will receive a compulsory offer of training, work or a combination.	Programmes for young people are being adapted as part of the response to the EU Youth Guarantee programme. Conditionality for young job seekers is the same as that for all the other job seekers.
To avoid the perpetuation of social exclusion and risk of poverty, put a stronger emphasis on encouraging and facilitating the return to work of those more detached from the labour market.	The focus on the long-term unemployed was renewed, and more resources are spent on the unemployed at most risk of becoming long-term unemployed identified through profiling.
To provide job-search assistance and activate the current cohort of long-term young unemployed, increase the number of caseworkers in the public employment service through internal redeployment.	300 staff were redeployed from other activities to activation duties.
Establish specific youth tracks in those schemes where youth are having access difficulties.	Such youth tracks have been introduced: for example: internships for disadvantaged youth in the JobBridge programme; access to recruitment subsidies eligible at shorter unemployment spells than for older unemployed in the JobsPlus programme.

Recommendations from previous *Survey*	Action taken since the October 2013 *Survey*
To respond to the demand for specialised skills, concentrate training efforts in those schemes providing high level skills such as Momentum, Springboard or ICT conversion courses. Progression pathways between different education levels should be stepped-up.	The Momentum programme is delivered in line with the Action Plan for Jobs and Pathways to Work. The 2nd phase of Momentum launched in 2014 aims to provide up to 6 000 education and training places for the long term unemployed, designed to tackle the skill shortages identified by the Expert Group on Future Skills Needs (EGFSN). Springboard+ 2015, which incorporates the ICT skills conversion programme was launched in May providing for a total of 9 000 free part-time and full time higher education reskilling and upskilling opportunities for jobseekers. 285 Springboard+ courses will be delivered in 42 colleges throughout Ireland. In 2014 Springboard provided over 5 700 places on 212 courses on part-time and full-time courses, including ICT Conversion courses.
To provide skilled workers to emerging sectors, expand the apprenticeship beyond craft-related areas involving the SME sector, better align curricula of vocational training to unemployed profiles and to employers demands and increase its workplace component.	The Apprenticeship Council was launched in November 2014. The council consists of representatives from business, trade unions, further education bodies and the Department of Education and Skills. It formally invited proposals for new apprenticeship programmes from consortia of enterprise, professional bodies and education and training providers. Over 80 separate proposals were received by the deadline
Establish a systematic and rigorous evaluation of all policies and schemes including sunset clauses to review at regular intervals the need for extensions. Based on the evaluation, reallocate resources to those schemes which are found to be effective in increasing employability.	A series of programme/process evaluations has been launched.
To adapt Pathways to Work to the changing structure of the Irish economy, establish a regular review and evaluation of the profiling model. Enlarge the model to encompass those more detached from the labour market.	The profiling model was reassessed, using administrative data, in 2013-14. There was little difference from the original model in terms of the factors predicting the severest difficulties in returning to employment. The re-assessed model has been used to estimate "distance from the labour market" scores for the existing long-term unemployed.
Establish a strategy to provide youth with relevant training and support. Introduce mentoring and coaching in the existing programme supporting self-entrepreneurship among unemployed.	The Back to Work Enterprise Allowance was implemented, which provides technical assistance grants for training/mentoring. See also other youth related actions above.
To reduce poverty risk and social exclusion, put a stronger emphasis on encouraging and facilitating the return to education or employment of those more unattached from the labour market by increasing mutual obligation approaches.	Reforms to lone parents' benefits are increasing conditionality of these payments where children are over 7 years of age.
Step-up the role and the capacity of psychological services to assist employment services in supporting young people and increase early childhood education as a preventive way to better integrate disfavoured youth.	Since the beginning of 2013 the number of educational psychologist staff within the National Educational Psychological Service (NEPS) has increased from 173 to 183. NEPS provides educational psychological service directly to all first and second level schools with schools in disadvantaged areas afforded priority service.
To realise its potential in the social inclusion of disadvantaged people, the social enterprise sector, including non-profits organisations, should be able to access the same kinds of government support as conventional enterprises.	No action.

Foster innovation and entrepreneurship

Recommendations from previous *Survey*	Action taken since the October 2013 *Survey*
Reflecting significant uncertainties about the effectiveness of various innovation policy tools, independently and regularly evaluate all actions in this area, strengthen programmes with proven higher returns, and wind down the others. To promote effective evaluation, ensure all innovation and enterprise supports have sunset clauses.	The Research and Development Tax Credit underwent an evaluation in 2013, while a review of enterprise supports for Research, Development and Innovation (RD&I) was completed in 2014. Regular independent evaluations of all RD&I programmes are undertaken. The recent mid-term review of the Enterprise Ireland/IDA Ireland Technology Centre programme recommended the sun-setting of two of the Technology Centres, and was actioned. Science Foundation Ireland (SFI) monitors its investments post-award.

Recommendations from previous *Survey*	Action taken since the October 2013 *Survey*
To increase the effectiveness and cost-efficiency of the innovation and research policies, and make it easier for businesses to access support, consolidate innovation funding and actions into a smaller number of Government agencies.	A National Directory of Research Centres was published with details of all centres of scale and their key areas of research.
To increase capital supply and encourage entrepreneurship, lower costs for small-cap IPOs, centralise legal processes for intellectual property rights (IPR) transfers with the new central technology transfer office and introduce changes to the examinership process without delay.	Knowledge Transfer Ireland (KTI), established in 2013, aims to make it easier for companies to access and use ideas developed through publicly-funded research. KTI provides a catalogue of practical guides including on License Agreements and Options Agreements to ensure a coherent approach across the system.
To improve Higher Education Institution (HEIs) quality, make a significant portion of their funding performance related, provide multi-year funding envelopes for HEIs, adjust their funding to reflect different student growth patterns across institutions and give them autonomy over staff salaries.	An expert group was established in 2014 to examine the current funding arrangements for higher education. In addition, a system of performance funding within core public funding of higher education was introduced in 2014.
To encourage MNCs to move advanced R&D functions to Ireland and build HEI-firm linkages, continue the strategy of building up fewer, larger academic research centres. Increase Masters and PhD graduates with significant firm placement components in order to provide firms, and particularly SMEs, with the innovation capacity to engage with HEIs. Further enhance SME-HEI links by setting up Research Technology Organisation/s targeting SME needs.	The Irish Research Council continues to develop its two enterprise scholarship schemes: the Employment Based Postgraduate and the Enterprise Partnership Scheme. Around 300 companies have engaged with the Council on these initiatives. SMEs account for more than 70% of the Partners engaging on the Employment- Based Programme. Twelve large scale research centres have been established. Some 300 industry partners are collaborating with the Centres and have committed funding. SFI funds the SFI Industry Fellowships, which facilitate the placement of researchers in industry or academia to stimulate knowledge transfer and training. A study has been undertaken on strengthening the market-focussed element of the research landscape in Ireland, including examination of establishing Research Technology Organisation/s.

Thematic chapters

© OECD 2015

Chapter 1

Growing together: Towards a more inclusive Ireland

The Irish economy is growing strongly, but there is a risk many households will be left behind despite robust growth. High joblessness especially among the low-educated and skill-biased wage differentials have induced high market income inequality, among the highest in the OECD. Ireland's comprehensive welfare system provides a broad range of social benefits, which keeps jobless households out of poverty, but this reduces the financial incentives to work, especially for families with children. Structural unemployment is also explained by the lack of skills required to find employment in the Irish labour market, where the presence of multinational enterprises increases the reward for high skills and the penalty for poor skills. With the unemployed pool lacking the right skills and financial incentives, employers tend to resort to foreign workers, a practice facilitated by the well-functioning migration system. Getting more people into work is important to share the benefits of the recovery as widely as possible. This requires building up work capacity, especially by improving jobseekers' training, and ensuring welfare recipients honour their Job Path commitments in return. More needs to be done to increase incentive to work by reducing welfare and low-income traps. This should be done by shifting the tax burden from labour to indirect taxes in a progressive way that does not harm the lowest income groups.

Ireland faces the challenge of having a high share of its population being unemployed or inactive, and thus receiving no labour earnings. High joblessness especially among the low-educated and large skill-biased wage differentials have induced high market income inequality. These features were already visible before the crisis, suggesting that the problem is largely structural. Although Ireland's welfare system provides a range of social transfers to reduce disposable income inequality and combat poverty, staying out of work for long periods of time undermines the well-being of families, with pervasive effects across generations. Getting more people back into work will therefore be key. To increase inclusion, while minimising distortions to growth, Ireland needs to:

- Facilitate the return to work of the unemployed by helping build-up work capacity, notably the acquisition of adequate skills, while making welfare conditional on beneficiaries honouring their Job-Path commitments.
- Improve the incentives to work by reducing welfare and income traps.
- Raising revenue more efficiently and equitably by continuing to shift the taxation burden away from labour taxes towards indirect taxes in a progressive way that does not harm the lowest income groups.

How inclusive is growth in Ireland?

Ireland's high structural unemployment and low labour-market participation results in large groups of households being left without labour income and relying almost exclusively on social transfers to make ends meet.

Figure 1.1. **Ireland's market income GINI is the highest in the OECD**

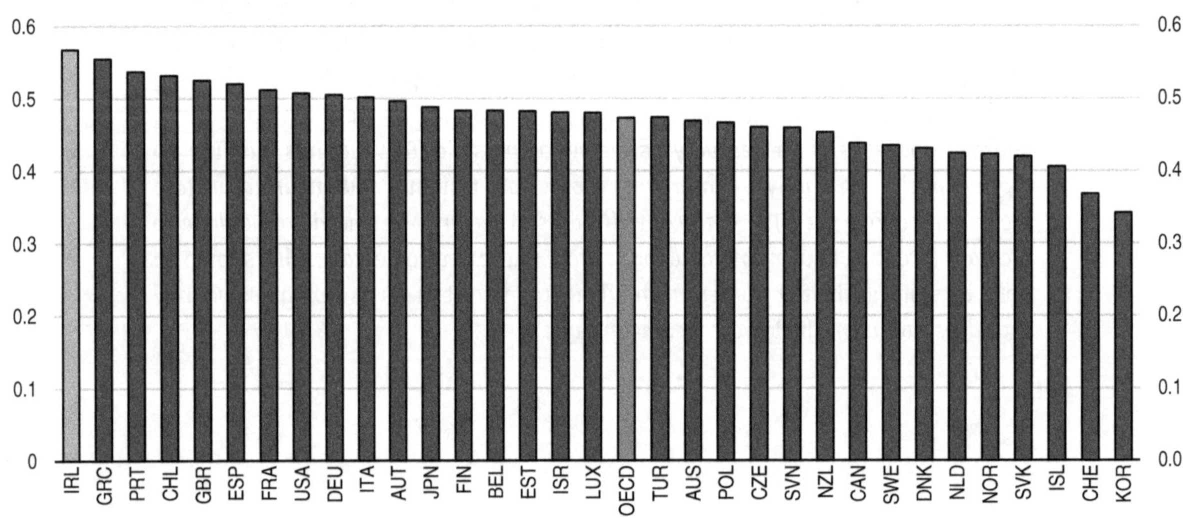

1. With 0 = perfect equality and 1 = perfect inequality.
Source: OECD Income Distribution Database.

StatLink http://dx.doi.org/10.1787/888933275173

OECD ECONOMIC SURVEYS: IRELAND © OECD 2015

This weakness of labour earnings at the bottom of the distribution results in income inequality being the highest in the OECD, when measured before taxes and transfers ("market incomes" GINI) (Figure 1.1). When taking into account taxes and transfers, however, Ireland's income inequality is below the OECD average (Figure 1.2), reflecting a tax and transfer system that is very effective in redistributing income. Indeed, the market income inequality increased markedly during the recession owing to the dramatic rise in employment losses (Figure 1.3). But after taxes and transfers inequality did not rise. This

Figure 1.2. **Ireland's disposable income GINI is below the OECD average**

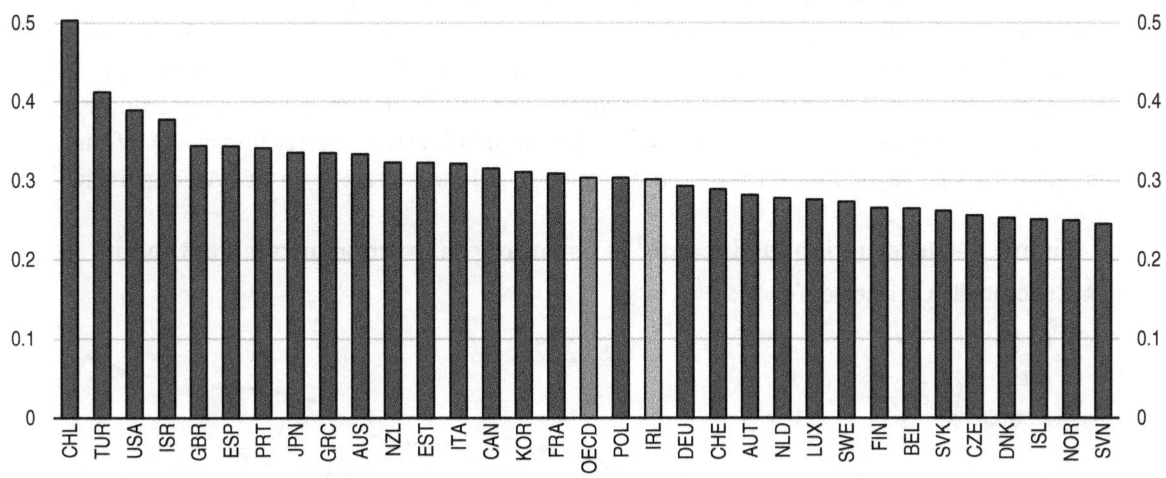

1. With 0 = perfect equality and 1 = perfect inequality.
Source: OECD Income Distribution Database.

StatLink http://dx.doi.org/10.1787/888933275180

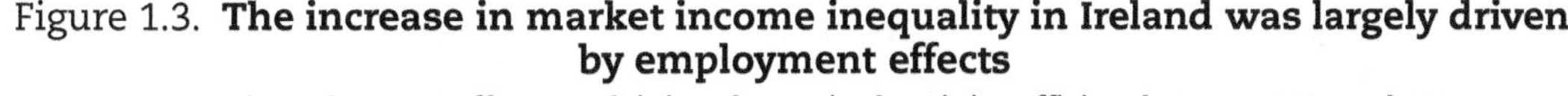

Figure 1.3. **The increase in market income inequality in Ireland was largely driven by employment effects**

Wage and employment effects explaining change in the Gini coefficient between 2007 and 2011

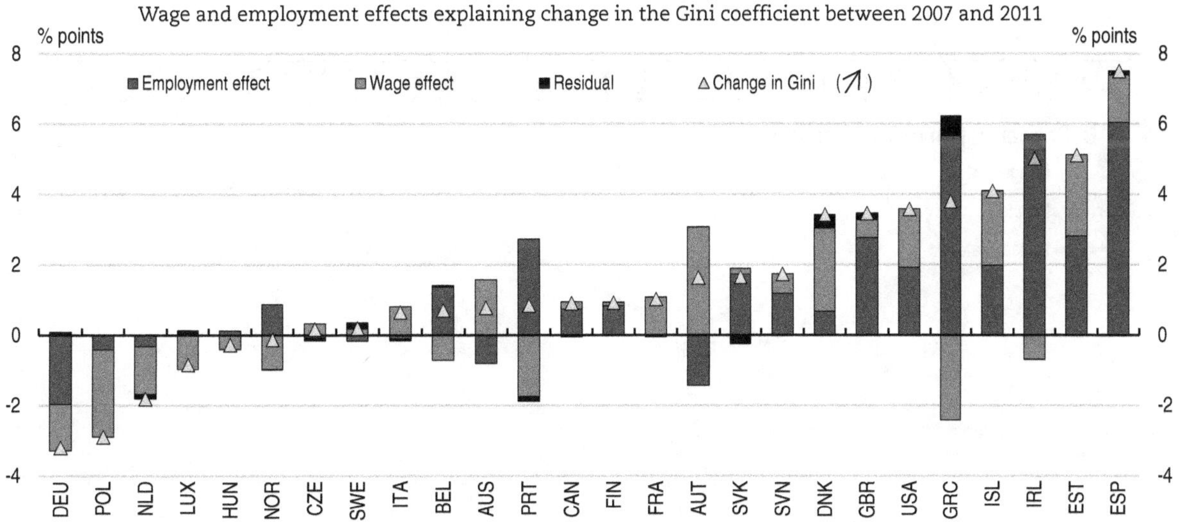

Source: OECD (2015), "In It Together: Why Less Inequality Benefits All", Chapter 3, Figure 3.2.

How to read this figure: The scale shows the change in the Gini index at market income between 2007 and 2011. This change is decomposed into wage and employment effects using the same method. For example, the market income inequality measured by the Gini index rose by some 5 percentage points in Ireland from 2007 to 2011, which is entirely explained by the employment effect (i.e. reduction in earnings following job separation was dominant), although the wage effect offset this very slightly (i.e. wage disparities among those in employment were reduced somewhat).

StatLink http://dx.doi.org/10.1787/888933275196

strong income support provided by the welfare system prevented the unemployed from falling into poverty, preserving economic and social stability.

Indicators of income concentration directly calculated from taxpayers' income statements to the Revenue Commissioners confirms that market income inequality is high in Ireland, driven by both ends of the income distribution. Around 37% of market income goes to the top 10% of tax units in 2012 (of which 10.5% and 3.3% to the top 1% and the top 0.1%, respectively, according to Kennedy et al., 2015). This concentration was somewhat lessened following the property bubble burst, but remains high. Nonetheless, by international comparison the concentration is not excessively high (Figure 1.4). High market income inequality is mostly driven by the lower end of the distribution: the income share of the bottom 20% households is the lowest in the OECD countries (Figure 1.5). A consequence of this is that at market incomes poverty is also very high. According to EU-SILC data, some 50% of individuals would live at or below the poverty line of 60% of the median disposable income, if they did not receive social transfers (Figure 1.6). Among those

Figure 1.4. **Internationally income[1] is becoming more concentrated at the top**

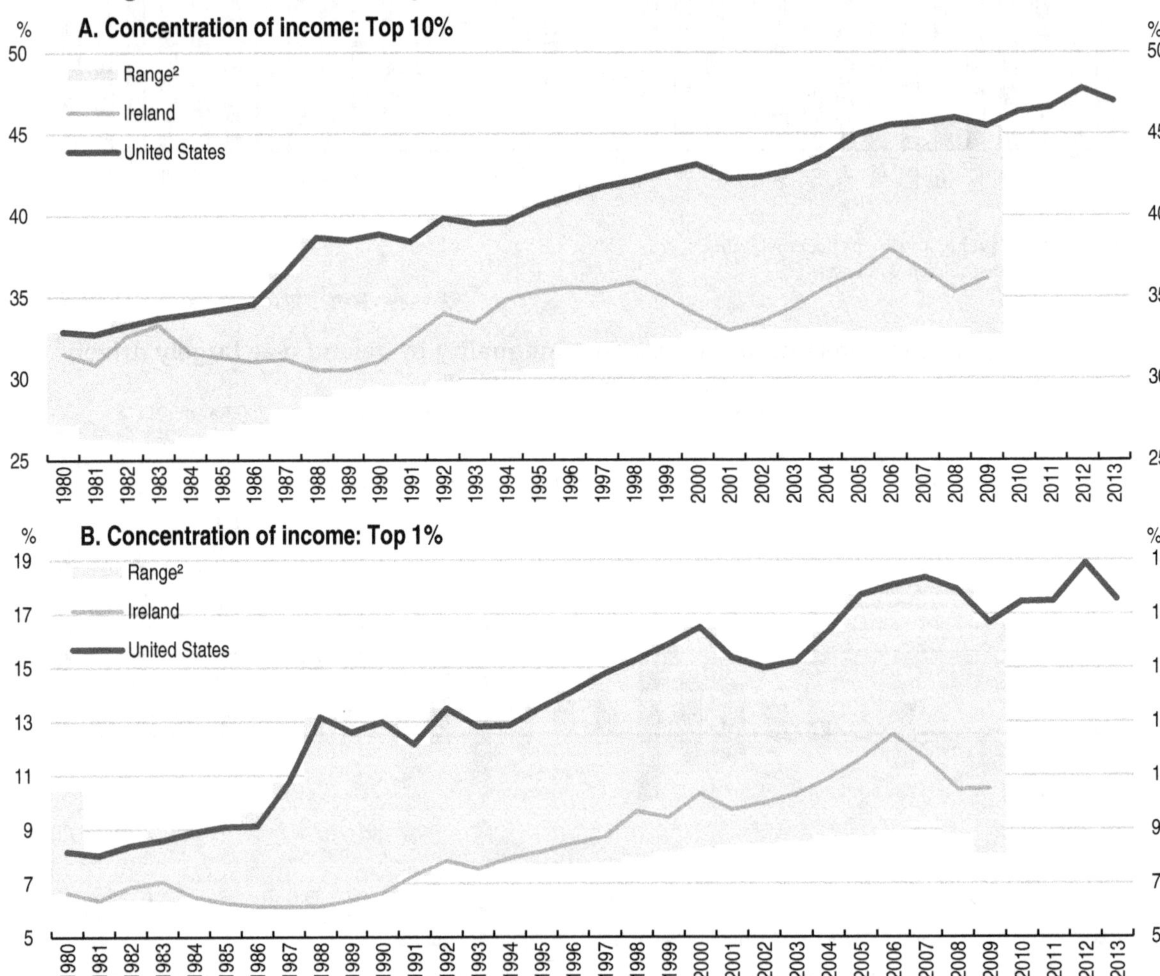

1. Market income.
2. The range is the difference between maximum and minimum value of France, Germany, Italy, United States, United Kingdom, Canada and Ireland.

Source: Alvaredo, Facundo, Anthony B. Atkinson, Thomas Piketty and Emmanuel Saez, *The World Top Incomes Database, http://topincomes.g-mond.parisschoolofeconomics.eu.*

StatLink http://dx.doi.org/10.1787/888933275202

Figure 1.5. **Share of the bottom 20% households in market income is low in Ireland**

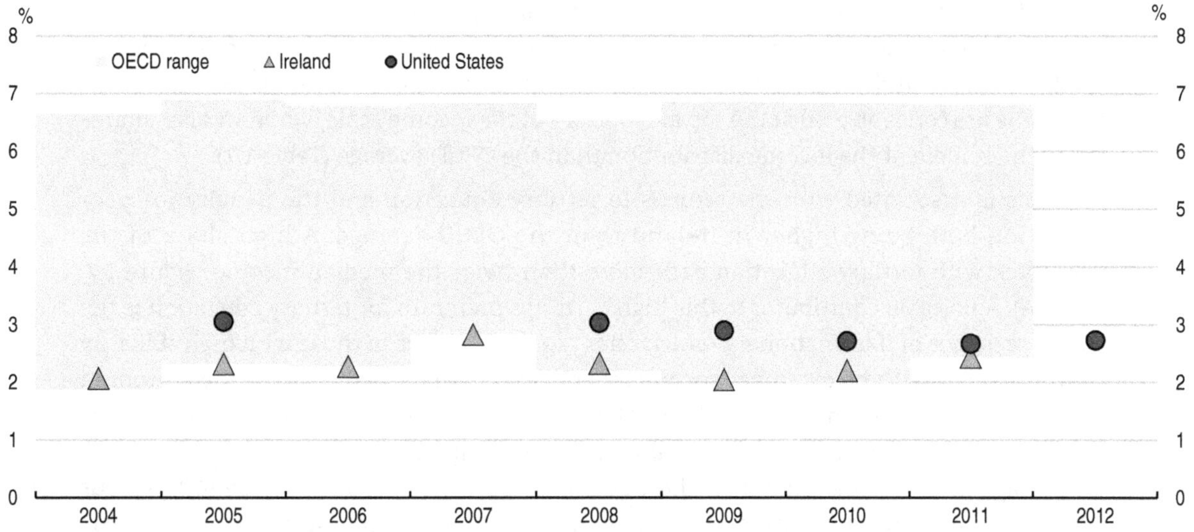

Source: OECD Secretariat's calculation from *OECD Income Distribution Database*.

StatLink http://dx.doi.org/10.1787/888933275217

Figure 1.6. **Risk of poverty is high without social transfers**

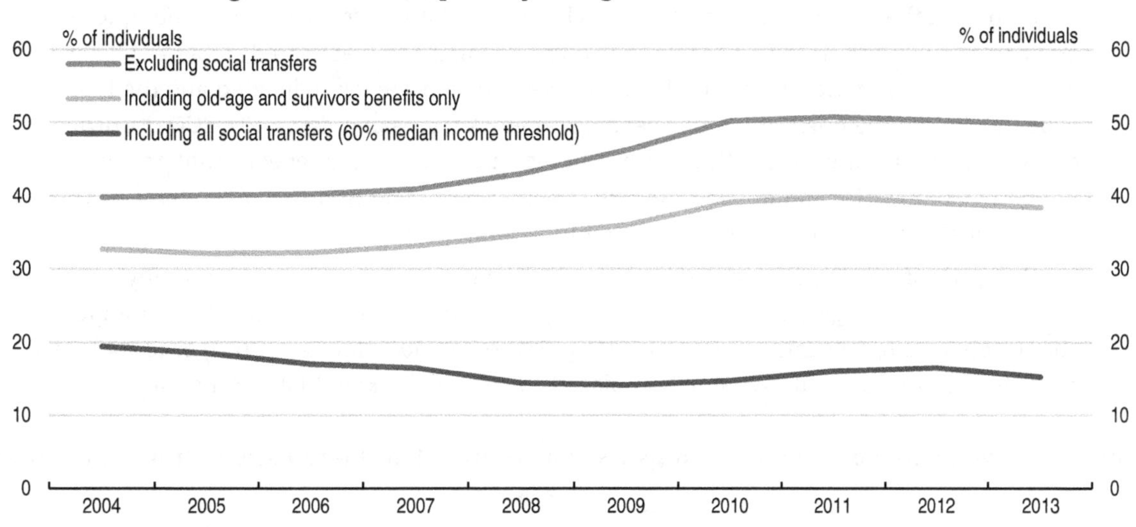

Source: Central Statistics Office, Ireland.

StatLink http://dx.doi.org/10.1787/888933275221

most affected by poverty are the unemployed (36.7%) and households where there is no person at work (34.5%).

Market income inequality is also strongly affected by macroeconomic fluctuations. During the early stages of the "Celtic tiger" period (1997-2002), all income groups experienced strong growth in market income (Kennedy et al., 2015). By contrast, when the economy entered into the property bubble (2002-07), only those at the top 9th decile and above benefitted, reflecting fast rise in both capital income and labour earnings at the high end of the income distribution. During the burst of the property bubble (2007-12), labour earnings declined by some 14% in the aggregate, with the burden disproportionately borne by those in lower income deciles.

Why is there such high inequality at market incomes?

Ireland's high inequality of market incomes largely reflects its uneven distribution of labour earnings. The ratio of the top income decile to the bottom income decile is high by OECD standards and the distribution has fatter tails than the OECD average. Higher shares of income are concentrated at the top and bottom of the income scale, while smaller shares are in the middle of the income distribution than the OECD average (Table 1.1).

This is associated with the returns to tertiary education and the penalty for poor education both being higher in Ireland than the OECD average. A high share of the workforce with tertiary education earn more than twice the median income (Figure 1.7, panel A). A possible contributor to this high earnings premium for tertiary education is the strong presence of multinationals, which offer highly-paid jobs to those with high skills. By contrast, those with below upper secondary education are concentrated at the bottom of the income distribution (Figure 1.7, panel B). These skill-based wage differentials have important effects on the overall distribution of earnings because Ireland has a higher percentage of 25-64 year olds than the OECD average with a tertiary degree (40% versus 33%) and about the same share of those with below upper secondary education as the OECD average of 24%.

There was a significant number of jobless households before the crisis, suggesting that unemployment has been a long-standing structural problem. Moreover, among those that are employed the share working part-time is high. The share of those who are unemployed or inactive, thus with no labour earnings, is high among the low-educated (Table 1.2). There was a marked difference in the employment rate between the low-educated and the high-educated before the crisis and it has become larger. A regression using 30 OECD countries to explain variations in the Gini before taxes and transfers suggests that the most important factors for Ireland are the low employment ratio and the high share of the tertiary qualified with a large earnings premium, which both raise inequality.

Labour's share of national income has declined in Ireland, as it has in many other OECD countries, largely reflecting technological changes (OECD, 2012): Technological change appears to be capital-augmenting (e.g. Bentolila and Saint-Paul, 2003) or to replace routine work (Autor et al., 2003) and is biased toward high-skilled labour (Bassanini and

Table 1.1. **High shares of labour earnings are concentrated at the top and bottom of the scale**

In per cent

	At or below half of the median	More than half the median but at or below the median	More than the median but at or below 1.5 times the median	More than 1.5 times the median but at or below twice the median	More than twice the median
Ireland					
Below upper secondary	40.0	27.8	17.9	9.5	4.8
Upper secondary or post-secondary non-tertiary	33.6	28.5	18.2	10.3	9.5
Tertiary-type B education	21.7	24.5	22.9	11.1	19.8
Tertiary-type A or advanced research programmes	13.8	15.4	14.4	19.3	37.2
All levels of education	27.4	24.3	17.8	12.7	17.9
OECD average					
Below upper secondary	27.1	46.3	19.0	4.8	2.7
Upper secondary or post-secondary non-tertiary	17.0	39.0	27.1	9.9	7.1
Tertiary-type B	12.3	27.4	31.5	15.1	13.7
Tertiary-type A or advanced research programmes	9.4	17.9	27.5	17.7	27.6
All levels of education	16.0	34.2	26.3	11.6	11.9

Source: OECD, *Education at a Glance.*

Figure 1.7. **Skill-based wage differentials are high in Ireland**

A. Percent of 25-65 year olds with tertiary education earning more than two times median income

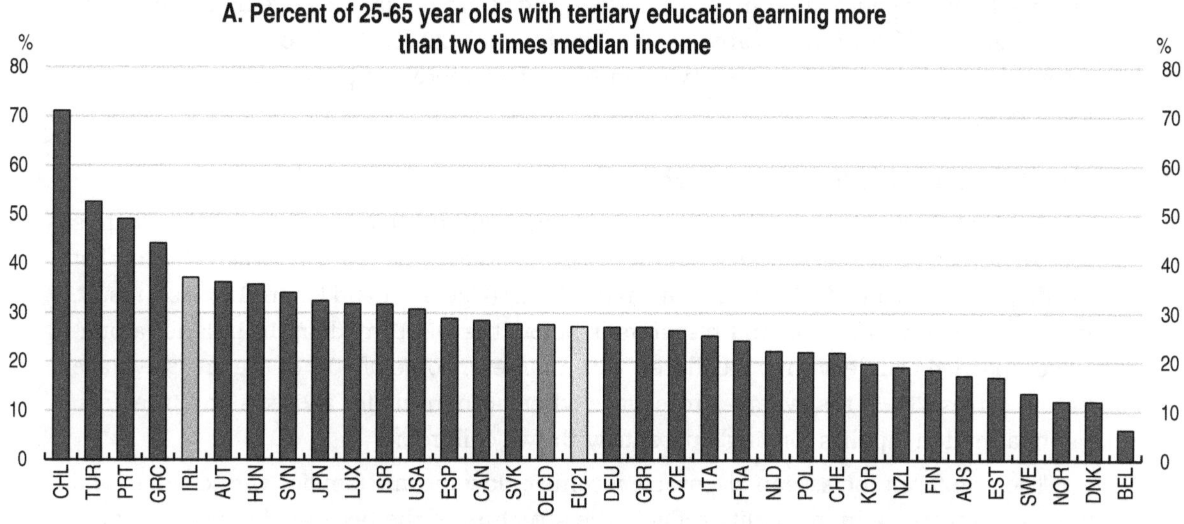

B. Percent of 25-65 year olds with below upper secondary education earning half or less of median income

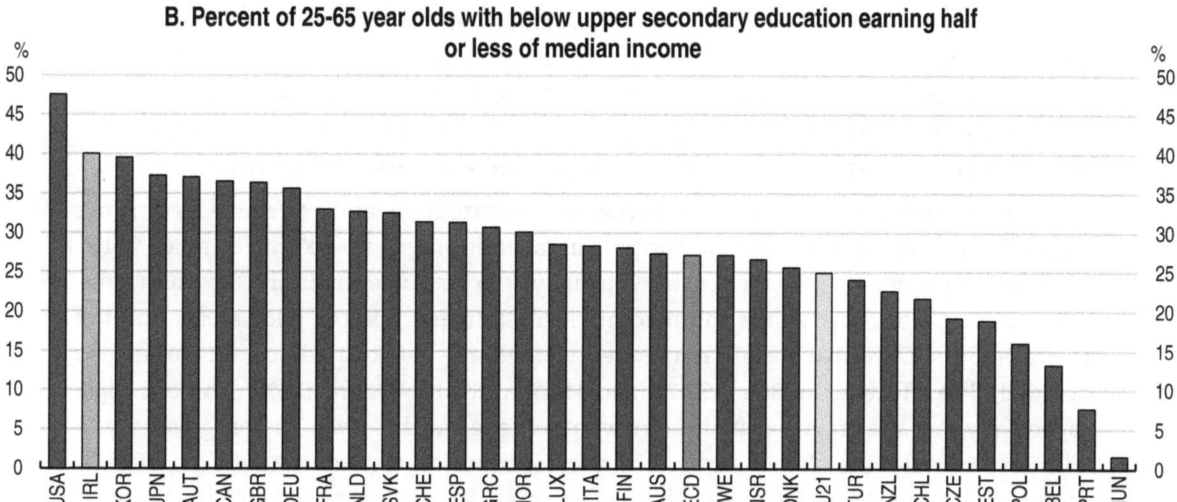

Source: OECD, *Education at a Glance*, 2014.

StatLink http://dx.doi.org/10.1787/888933275236

Table 1.2. **The low-educated are more likely to be jobless than the OECD average**

Employment rate by educational attainment level, in per cent

	2000	2005	2010	2013
Ireland				
Below upper secondary	55.9	58.4	47.6	46.9
Upper secondary or post-secondary non-tertiary	76.6	76.7	66.5	66.0
Tertiary education	87.5	86.8	81.0	80.1
OECD average				
Below upper secondary	57.2	56.5	55.5	54.7
Upper secondary or post-secondary non-tertiary	75.1	74.8	73.8	73.5
Tertiary education	84.7	84.1	83.1	83.0

Source: Education at a Glance Interim Report (OECD, 2015).

Manfredi, 2012). Also, globalisation has raised pressures to reduce labour costs, due to increased import penetration from, and offshoring of production to, developing countries (OECD, 2007; Hijzen and Swaim, 2010; Bloom et al, 2011). Such pressures are felt particularly by low-skilled workers, who in effect face more competition from workers in developing countries.

How does Ireland reduce inequality?

For Irish families with children, the tax and welfare system provides an effective system of income redistribution, as shown by the largest difference between the market and disposable income GINI coefficients in the OECD (Figure 1.1 and Figure 1.2). As a result, income inequality after tax and transfers is below the OECD median. In Ireland, a one-earner married couple with two children with market income of 50% of the gross average wage receives 85% of the average gross wage when accounting for all taxes and transfers. A similar pattern applies for single parents with two children.

The significant increase in disposable income of low-income families with children and associated decrease in inequality reflects the structure of the tax-transfer system: these families pay low or zero income taxes and social charges; and they receive significant welfare payments related to housing, child or replacement income. By international standards, Ireland provides generous social family income support. Direct child income support has three main components: Qualified Child Increases (QCIs) targeted at welfare recipients, Family Income Supplement (FIS) targeted at low-income employees and a universal child benefit.

Social transfers are funded by a progressive tax system. Ireland's effective income tax rate, defined as the share of total income paid in taxes, is progressive (Kennedy et al., 2015). The effective income tax rate ranges from virtually zero for taxpayers in the lowest income decile to 30.9% for those in the top income decile (income tax, tax allowances and tax credits, and the Universal Social Charge are included; the Pay Related Social Insurance is excluded). The effective tax rate is 38.2% and 41.1% at the top 1% and 0.1% income groups, respectively, and the progressivity is somewhat lessened at this level. The progressivity in the Irish tax system is also confirmed by the contribution to total tax receipts of each income decile. In 2012, 59.3% of income tax revenue was paid by the top 10% tax units (of which 21.3% and 7.2% for the top 1% and 0.1% tax units, respectively).

New data compiled for this *Economic Survey* shows that Ireland's tax and welfare system has become increasingly more supportive of low- and middle- income households. The total amount of social benefits on which tax has been paid (around ¼ of total social benefits) has risen significantly as it has been more than doubled as a percentage of disposable income over the last decade. While tax credits have become more generous for low and middle-income households, tax allowances were reduced for high-income earners. As a result, after-tax income is more evenly distributed and its share is increased up to the 8th decile (transfers especially benefit the 3rd to 6th income deciles, while the tax system overall supports the 2nd to 7th). Higher income groups bear most of the tax burden. For the top decile, the share of market income is 36.8%, but 29.7% after taxes and transfers. However, the reduction in the share of income after redistribution is less pronounced for the top 1% and above.

Social mobility is low at the low end of distribution

Social mobility (the probability of individuals changing income group over time) is also an important aspect of inclusiveness. In a mobile society, households can move up (or down) relatively fast, while this is not the case in an immobile society. A high level of income inequality is of more concern if coupled with low mobility across time. From the perspective of inclusiveness, it is a particular concern if those who are at the low end of income distribution remain stuck overtime. Such immobility is very likely to arise from high incidence of long-term inactivity, possibly associated with low incentives to return to work due to welfare dependence.

New data compiled for this *Economic Survey* shows that about 43% of tax units remained in the same quintile income groups between 2004 and 2012 (Kennedy et al., 2015). Less mobility occurs at the low and high ends of income distribution (47% and 58% of tax units remained in the lowest and highest quintile groups), while mobility is more frequent in middle income classes (on average 37% of tax units remained in the same quintile group). This is similar to the United States. The mobility at the lowest end of income distribution increased during the crisis as more people crowded into that group after losing their job and main source of income (which resulted in comparative and incremental upward mobility of the rest of the population).

Wealth tends to be more unevenly distributed than income, and even more so if coupled with income immobility. There is an apparent correlation between the wealth and income distribution and wealth is particularly concentrated at the higher end of the income distribution (Table 1.3). The way financial assets are distributed is consistent with the fact that capital income is concentrated among the highest income groups (Kennedy et al, 2015). The factors explaining income disparity are also reflected in the wealth

Table 1.3. **Assets are distributed unevenly across income and socio-economic groups**

Median value of wealth for each group as a share of the overall median value in the economy

	Any real assets	Any financial assets
Percentile of income		
< 20	0.62	0.48
20-39	0.63	0.37
40-59	0.94	0.68
60-79	1.12	1.37
80-100	1.84	4.92
Work status of reference person		
Employee	0.97	0.95
Self-employed	2.13	4.29
Retired	1.12	1.90
Unemployed	0.50	0.16
Other	0.88	0.49
Education of reference person		
Primary education or lower	0.82	0.79
Lower secondary	0.93	0.67
Upper and post-secondary	0.98	0.79
Third level degree and lower	1.22	1.68
Postgraduate	1.22	2.38

Note: The reported median value in each socio-economic group is the median value among the households with any assets. CSO (2015) reports data by each socio-economic group (income quintile, region, household size, educational attainment, employment status) in terms of: percentage of households owning any kind of assets (main residence, other properties, lands, deposits, equities, bonds, etc.); median value of these assets conditional on ownership (i.e. excluding the households without assets); and the share of each assets within each socio-economic group. "Reference person" is the person who answered the survey question in each household.

Source: CSO (2015), from the results from the Household Finance and Consumption Survey 2013 which provides details of the household financial situation according to different household types, including income and wealth.

distribution: highly educated people tend to own more assets than the rest; the unemployed people have typically much lower wealth than those in employment (Table 1.3). The high level of market income inequality associated with low income mobility, if it cumulates over time, will further increase wealth disparities. This in turn may lay ground for perpetuating further disparities: those who were born in less wealthier households attain lesser degrees of education, affecting their income prospects.

Towards more inclusive growth

Ireland needs to shore up its future growth prospects by ensuring the benefits of the recovery are spread widely. The first priority should be to get more people into better paying jobs. This requires building skills among the unemployed and continuing to improve activation policies in line with best-practice centred on mutual obligations. The business sector has an important role to play in both these endeavours through its input into training design and providing on-the-job training opportunities as part of apprenticeship and other programmes. Ireland also needs to reduce existing disincentives to work that are built in the tax and welfare system. The system does a generally good job at supporting those on lower incomes, but a side-effect of the system is that the beneficiaries of social transfers may face high effective marginal tax rates upon return to work, or once in work when they want to increase their hours.

Building skills and getting more people back into work

An important policy implication of the labour earnings distribution is that for Ireland, even more than for most OECD countries, reducing inequality at market incomes requires lifting education levels of the most poorly educated. This requires upgrading the skills of the unemployed, particularly the long-term unemployed and preventing youth from leaving the education system under-qualified. One of the key elements in designing policies to get people back to work is conditionality (discussed further below), that is, providing benefits conditional on the recipient actively searching for work, taking an available job, or taking training (OECD, 2013a).

Around 90 000 persons, i.e. 26% of the registered unemployed, have been without a job for more than 3 years, and only 51% of single parents were in employment in 2014, compared to an EU15 average of 69%; the latter gap was apparent before the crisis, indicating that it is largely structural. In addition, many workers who lost their jobs, especially men and older workers, have stopped seeking a job and withdrawn altogether from the labour market (Kelly et al., 2015). The activity rates of the low-skilled are particularly low in Ireland. Only 50% of the individuals in the 20-30 age group are employed or are seeking work, 20 percentage points lower than in other advanced economies in the European Union.

Ireland has a markedly higher percentage of younger cohorts (25-34 years old) with tertiary qualifications than both OECD and EU averages. However, there remains a large cohort of unemployed with insufficient skills. Raising skill levels is especially important for reducing inequality at market incomes given the mentioned evidence that the reward for education and the penalty for a lack of skills are very high. These high skill premiums and penalties result from the wide gap between the skills of the workforce and the needs of employers (Figure 1.8): employers are willing to pay a premium for hard-to-find talents, but are unwilling to do so for the many with low skills. This gap is increasing: the recovery is

Figure 1.8. **Skill mismatches are high**

Percentage of workers with skill mismatches; selected OECD countries, 2011-12

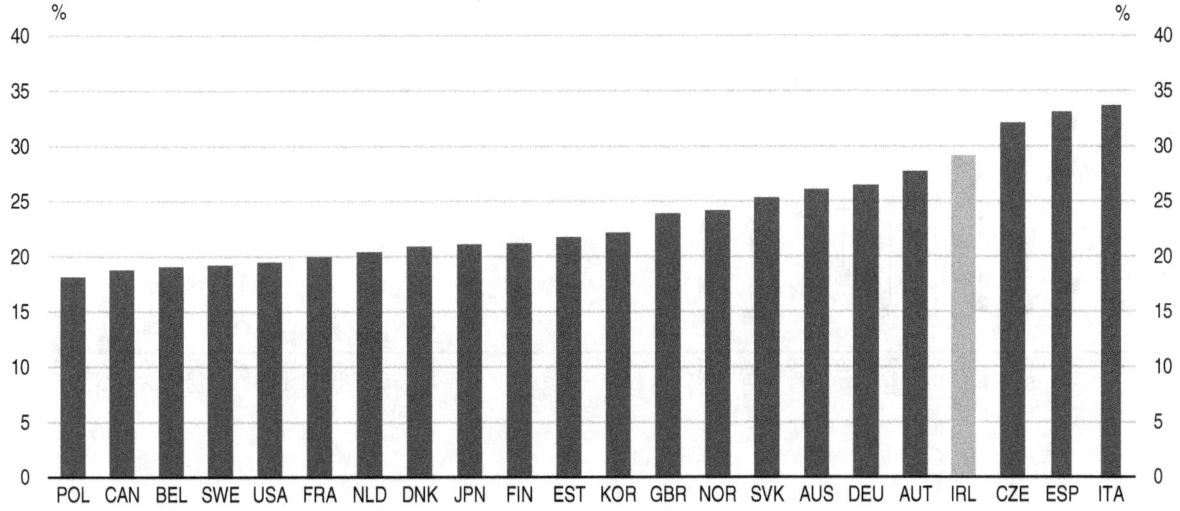

Source: Adalet-McGowan and Andrews (2015) based on OECD PIAAC data.

StatLink http://dx.doi.org/10.1787/888933275249

skill-intensive and creates job opportunities mostly for high-skilled workers, exacerbating the existing situation.

As elsewhere in the world, Ireland has significant ICT skill gaps, with a low proportion of the population attaining good ICT skills. This ICT skills distribution translates into very large wage differentials. The salary of those with good ICT skills is more than 200% higher than the salary of those without ICT skills (OECD, 2014). This gap is one of the largest observed in the OECD. It reflects that demand for these skills is very high in Ireland. While the domestic supply of ICT graduates is ramping up, more than half of the companies that attempted to recruit ICT professionals reported difficulties finding those skills (Eurostat, 2014). Encouragingly the percentage of ICT graduates in total tertiary graduates is rising and the Department of Education has put in place an ICT action plan with the aim of further increasing the domestic supply of ICT graduates to 74% of demand by 2018. Other occupations where supply needs to increase include engineering, science and health, as well as multilingual sales and customer care roles.

The OECD Survey of Adult Skills (PIAAC) signals that despite improvements in recent years, Irish adults' skill level is significantly below the OECD average, and in the bottom quintile, both in numeracy and literacy skills. This relatively poor performance is partly explained by those aged 45 to 65, who on average have relatively low levels of educational attainment. However, according to PIAAC, younger people in Ireland also compared unfavourably with their peers in other OECD countries (Figure 1.9). The percentage of younger adults scoring at higher proficiency levels is low in Ireland in international comparison.

Beyond up-skilling the adult population, an equally fundamental challenge is ensuring that Irish youth acquire the skills needed to succeed in a more knowledge intensive economy. Positive developments are visible on that front. Ireland has made good progress in improving the skills of students in compulsory education as measured by PISA and has also succeeded in having a lower than average dropout rate and higher completion rates.

Figure 1.9. **A low proportion of adults have high-level skills**

Percentage of younger and older adults scoring at PIAAC literacy proficiency Level 4 or 5 (2012)

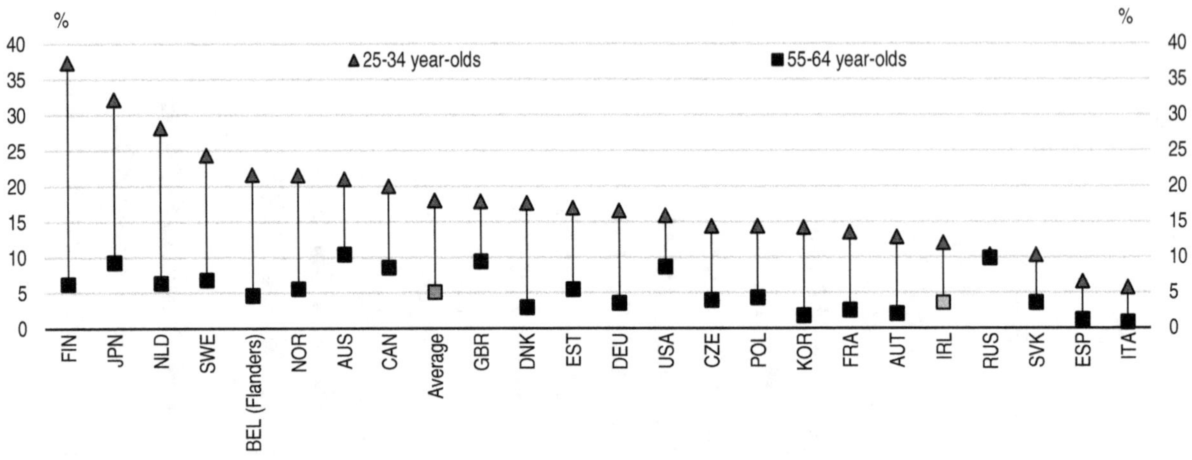

Source: OECD PIAAC, OECD (2014).

StatLink http://dx.doi.org/10.1787/888933275252

In tertiary education, the challenge is to ensure that skills gained in education can be efficiently transferred to the labour market. Steps have been taken to improve the alignment between the output from universities and the needs of industry, but more could be done. Improving existing information about labour market status and wages of graduates would be a useful step to provide further guidance for students. Wage information could be obtained by matching graduation and social security records. Information should encompass both university graduates and also holders of vocational and technical degrees. Providing all this information to students could be an important device to create demand-side pressure for greater labour market relevance of education programmes and could also eventually improve the reputation of vocational and technical options, which tend to have a lower social status than university studies. Ensuring that students receive appropriate information on all educational options available to them after school, including vocational and technical options, would also facilitate transitions to work and help to reduce skill mismatches.

Another important factor for Ireland becoming more skills inclusive is to minimise the impact that socio-economic status has on educational opportunities. There is evidence of social inequalities in higher education participation in Ireland. Young people from working-class backgrounds are less likely to go on to higher education than their middle-class peers and are also more likely to be unemployed upon leaving school. There is also evidence that the school social mix has a strong effect on educational outcomes (McCoy et al., 2014). More than 75% of the performance differences observed between schools are explained by the socio-economic status of students and schools (OECD, 2013b). Providing disadvantaged schools with additional support, for example attracting the best teachers by paying them more or providing additional tutoring help, and making school choice policies more conducive to mixed social backgrounds would make Irish educational system more socially inclusive.

Using active labour market policies to boost employment

Activation services, including training providing participants with new and relevant skills, are crucial to boost employment prospects of the low-skilled unemployed. Progress in upgrading labour market activation policies in Ireland towards best practices in OECD countries has continued. The number of jobseekers that each caseworker in the Public Employment Services oversees on average has fallen from 800 in 2013 to 500. This is still at the higher end in international comparison and well above what is considered best practice.

The education and training system is being reformed. SOLAS, the agency in charge of overseeing the delivery of further education and the training to the unemployed, was established in October 2013. In 2014, SOLAS prepared the first ever integrated "Further Education and Training (FET) Service Plan". The plan documents the full range of FET provision and its costs. SOLAS will need to ensure that the FET programme meets the evolving needs of unemployed and of employers.

The apprenticeship system, narrowly geared towards the construction sector and hardly used by women, is also being reformed. Nevertheless, the pace of reform is very slow and lags behind the reform pace in other areas. Eight years after the start of the crisis and the construction bust, the development of the new apprenticeship system is only beginning. An apprenticeship council was established in November 2014. A call for proposals to develop apprenticeships in areas beyond construction trades, as recommended in previous *Economic Surveys* (for example OECD, 2011; OECD, 2013b), was issued in January 2015. Proposals were received by the end of March 2015, and the apprenticeship council will evaluate them by the end of June.

The authorities are rolling-out the *JobPath* initiative, whereby private providers will be in charge of activating the long-term unemployed. The actual service provision will only start in the second part of 2015. International evidence signals that, frequently, there are difficulties in implementing effectively the contracting out of activation. A successful roll-out will be crucial to avoid the current cohort of long-term unemployment becoming perpetually disenfranchised from the labour market and socially excluded.

Ireland devotes significant fiscal resources to active labour market programmes intended to assist the unemployed getting back to work by international standards (Gonzalez Pandiella, 2013). Some new programmes aimed at providing relevant skills to Ireland's increasingly knowledge-intensive economy have been launched. These programmes include *Momentum* (vocational education for the long-term unemployed) and *Springboard* (full and part-time courses in higher education for the unemployed), among others. Although such programmes are found to show good potential, they still account for a relatively low share of the overall total training envelope.

The emphasis should be thus on ensuring that those resources are channelled towards programmes and schemes that proved to be effective in helping people to gain employment. For that it is essential that evaluation mechanisms are put in place to determine what really works and, accordingly, reallocate resources towards programmes and training schemes improving employment prospects and shut down ineffective ones. Post-programme evaluation is well established across different government departments but there is room to make the evaluation more rigorous (see for example O'Connell, 2015 and Denny, 2015). Progress has been made in setting-up the data infrastructure to collect and link information on participants and outcomes. This information should be used to undertake timely statistical evaluation of the training programmes.

One of the few rigorous evaluations conducted in recent years that employed a control group found that some training programmes do indeed enhance the subsequent employment prospects of their participants (McGuinness et al., 2014). The study found strong employment effects for job-search skills training and medium to high level skills courses. The same study also found more modest effects for lower-level skills training, which possibly resulted from lack of policy coordination: less intensity of job search obligation and generous welfare payments (OECD, 2013a).

Effective implementation of conditionality is required

An important part of best practice active labour market policies is effectively implementing mutual obligations. Conditionality should complement adequate welfare support in order to encourage people to return to work. As the economy recovers and jobs availability increases jobseekers obligations in return for the training and other support provided by the Public Employment Service can be strictly enforced.

In the 2000s, the sanction rate for refusal of work in Ireland was close to the lowest among OECD countries, while that for insufficient job search was about 0.7% of the stock of benefit recipients – below the level for countries that required similar reporting on job-search actions (OECD, 2013a). McGuiness et al. (2011) show, with Irish data on unemployment benefit recipients, that those who do not actively commit to such activities, without effective control, encounter lower chances of entering employment.

Conditionality for unemployment benefits was tightened under "Pathways to Work" labour market reforms introduced in the early 2010s (OECD, 2013b). The percentage of beneficiaries penalised for non-compliance has increased since then. The sanction is applied gradually, beginning with a temporary reduction (around 25%) to a suspension up to 9 weeks. The sanction rate for those who failed to attend two initial interviews with the public employment service was 3.2% (of the inflow to the recipients) in 2014, which seems to be comparable with other OECD countries. The sanction for those who refuse to commit to active job search amounted to some 9200 cases, which is estimated to be around 3.0% of those who are registered as unemployed.

The conditionality approach can be even more enhanced in setting some objective criteria, as currently the sanction for non-compliance seems to be decided at the caseworker's discretion. For instance, the job seeker can be sanctioned when refusing a suitable job offer, against such criteria as wages, working hours, contract types, location, etc. However, it is not entirely clear how the job seeker is judged to decline a "suitable" job offer (for example, in which circumstances the job seeker has to accept a temporary contract, or what would be considered the maximum acceptable reduction of the wage compared with the previous job, etc.). The conditions do not necessarily have to be defined relative to the previous job but some objective criteria would help to motivate the job seeker/recipient of benefits to accept a job.

The provision of social benefits (other than unemployment benefits) is not now subject to conditionality in Ireland, even though many of beneficiaries could be considered fit for work. While such conditionality is not appropriate for all benefits, the authorities should consider the extent to which it could be extended.

Welfare payments and work incentives

The Irish welfare system succeeds generally well in protecting the long-term unemployed and inactive from poverty, thus keeping income inequality near the OECD average. The overall transfer system is generous by international standards, as measured by the large decline in inequality due to transfers. In addition to allowances for jobseekers, Ireland provides a variety of welfare benefits related to housing, children and incentives to return to work.

Achieving re-distributional goals, while ensuring the tax and welfare system disincentives to work are minimised, is a tricky balancing exercise with many constraints. A key challenge is to deliver acceptable incomes for those earning no or low market income, while maintaining the incentive to work. The overall cost of the system is also a key consideration from a fiscal perspective and limits how far it is possible to go in minimising disincentive effects of the tax and welfare system – it is possible to lower disincentive effects by having slow or no (i.e. universal) abatement rates for benefits, but this is expensive.

Fostering inclusive growth through fairer and more efficient welfare and taxation

The design of the tax and welfare system directly affects incentives to work and to hire and therefore has a large bearing on employment outcomes and market income inequality. Labour taxes tend to be more harmful to growth and employment than property taxes (Johansson et al., 2008, Arnold et al., 2011). By creating a wedge between the cost to the employer and the gain to the employee they are a disincentive to hire and to supply labour, and therefore reduce employment and increase inequality. In Ireland there is potential to carry out a growth, jobs and equality enhancing shift in the tax system away from labour taxation towards property taxation as well as broadening the tax base. Ireland's high reliance on the tax and transfer system for reducing inequality means that such a shift needs to be designed carefully in order to avoid the shift being regressive.

Simulations show such a shift, if designed carefully, can be done in a progressive way that promotes growth inclusively (O'Connor et al., 2015). This requires examining micro-data based evidence of where welfare and low-income traps exist and how policy changes would affect the income and incentives of households across the income distribution. Previous work shows that relying on only a few example representative households to illustrate the effects of tax and welfare changes can be misleading (Callan et al., 2012). The following section is based on analysing the income implications and incentives facing individuals using micro-data (household survey data) simulations of tax and benefit policies in the Economic and Social Research Institute's (ESRI) tax-benefit SWITCH model carried out in O'Connor et al. (2015), as well as in previous literature.

Reducing welfare traps

For large parts of the population the tax and welfare system maintains a strong incentive to shift from welfare to work. Indeed around two-thirds of the unemployed are single and therefore receive only the Job Seekers Benefit (JSB) or Job Seekers Allowance (JSA). Single individuals on both JSB and JSA tend to have low replacement rates (Savage et al., 2015).

However, there is evidence that unemployment traps do exist in Ireland for some groups, and particularly for those with a non-working partner and children (Savage et al., 2015). Around 18% of the unemployed in receipt of a JSB or JSA have a replacement rate of 70% and above. The main causes for this are means tested child benefits (Increases for a Qualified Child, IQC), means tested payments for a non-working or low income partner (Increases for a Qualified Adult, IQA) and housing-cost-related payments. Indeed, simulations with micro data shows that 39% of the unemployed with children face a replacement rate of over 70% compared to only 6% of those without children (Savage et al., 2015).

However, reducing these high replacement rates by cutting IQC and IQA payments is undesirable as it would substantially increase the depth of poverty, given that these payments are closely targeted at the lowest income households (Savage et al., 2014). An alternative is to ensure than in-work benefits at least partially compensate for the withdrawal of IQCs and IQAs. The new *Back to Work Family Dividend* introduced in 2015 that replaces the IQC fully in the first year of work and 50% of the IQC in the second year is designed to help do this but the overall package of in-work benefits needs to be re-examined. These benefit types require careful design as an in-work low income supplement designed to reduce a high replacement rate can end up creating a low income trap if the abatement rate is high (Callan et al., 2012). This appears to be the case with the Family Income Supplement (FIS) discussed below.

The rent and mortgage supplement (RMS) has also been a factor in high replacement rates (Savage et al., 2014). An important reason for this was that RMS used to be unavailable to a person working more than 30 hours a week. This problem is being tackled with the new housing assistance payment (HAP), which is replacing the rent supplement part of RMS. The legislation underpinning HAP was enacted in 2014 and it has been rolled out to circa 2 300 households so far with targets to further increase households covered. HAP is a social housing support and is therefore available to households that qualify for social housing support. Eligibility for social housing support is based on income and housing need and does not depend on hours worked removing the potential barrier to move into work. To reduce the disincentive to return to work, the government should ensure all housing assistance payments depend on income rather than employment status.

Reducing low income traps

Even if someone exits unemployment to work, high METRs (percentage of an income increase absorbed by taxes, charges and benefit reductions) can act as a disincentive, creating low-income traps where someone's net monetary incentive to work more is low. The personal tax wedge is made of an income tax, and two types of social security contributions, an income levy (the Universal Social Charge, USC) and a social security contribution (the Pay-Related Social Insurance, PRSI). The latter is a paid by both employees and employers. The universal social charge is payable once annual income exceeds EUR 12 000 with a maximum rate of 8% for PAYE earners and 11% for non-PAYE earners. There are only two income tax bands: 20% on incomes up to EUR 33 800 (around the average wage) for single taxpayers and 40% thereafter. There are two main income tax credits, a personal income tax credit for all taxpayers in the state and a Pay As You Earn (PAYE) tax credit for salary, wage and pension earners. The result of these two credits is that no income tax is paid on incomes under EUR 16 500. They are the two most expensive tax credits (Kennedy et al., 2015). In addition there are employee social security contributions (PRSI) of 4% that are payable from an income of EUR 18 304 (for more details on the tax bands, see O'Connor et al., 2015).

On this basis Ireland maintains low average effective tax rates on the low paid by international comparison and an average effective tax rate around the OECD average for the higher paid (Figure 1.10). However, the system generates undesirable jumps in marginal effective tax rates at some points in the income distribution, even for those without children (Figure 1.11). At the bottom end of the income distribution the main issues are spikes in the marginal effective tax rate that occur as a taxpayer becomes liable, first for the USC at EUR 12 012, then at around EUR 16 500-18 000 (approximately 57% of the average wage) when they become liable for income tax and then employee social security contributions. The first priority should be to reduce these spikes in marginal tax wedge, to prevent threshold impediments to supplying more labour. The spikes could be smoothed without raising the average effective tax wedge by using lower tax credits and more

Figure 1.10. **Average tax wedge is low for the low paid and close to the OECD average for the higher paid**

Single person no child, 2014

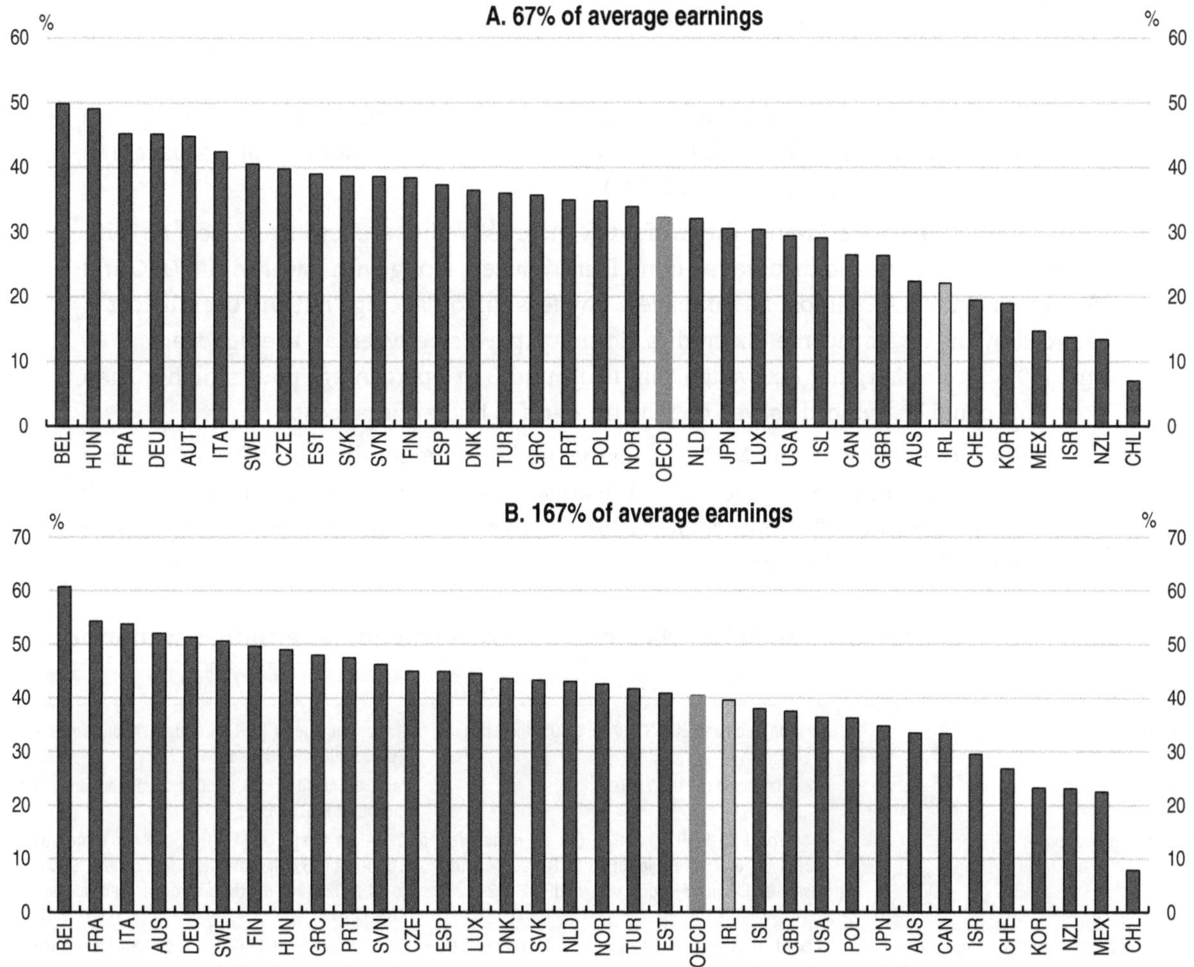

Source: *OECD Taxing Wages Database.*

StatLink http://dx.doi.org/10.1787/888933275262

Figure 1.11. **Some undesirable jumps in the marginal effective tax rate are built into the current system**

Total marginal effective tax rates 2015 (single, no children)

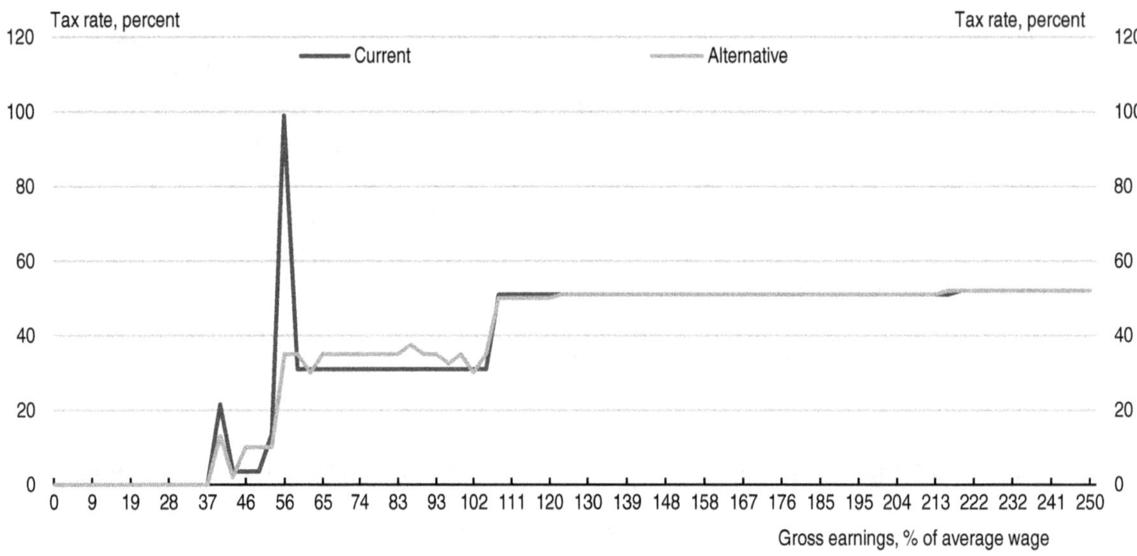

Source: OECD *Taxing Wages*, Revenue Commissioners and author calculations.

StatLink http://dx.doi.org/10.1787/888933275270

gradually rising income tax, USC and PRSI rates. A rough estimate of the cost of this policy based on multiplying the gain at different income deciles by the number of tax payers in each decile is EUR 300 million (0.16% of GDP).

In the alternative scenario, the initial tax income credits are lower and decline with income and a three band income tax band is introduced, along with lower initial USC and PRSI rates (Table 1.4). Almost all tax payers pay less tax on average but the overall cost is reduced by the lower income tax credits. Some taxpayers between an average wage of 60 and 100% face a marginal tax wedge that is around 3 to 4 percentage points higher than now. This could be reduced as well but the trade-off is higher fiscal cost.

Beyond the spikes in the METR at low wage levels generally, some lower income households with children face additional disincentives to work due to the way in-work benefits are withdrawn. The principal reason for this is the Family Income Supplement (FIS). FIS was introduced to provide an incentive to move from welfare to work (AGTSW,

Table 1.4. **Tax rates and bands for PAYE taxpayers: Actual and alternative scenarios**

	Actual	Alternative
Income tax rates	20% on income to EUR 33 800 and 40% thereafter.	9% on income to EUR 18 000, 20% on remainder to EUR 33 800, 40% thereafter.
Income tax credit	Fixed Tax credit of EUR 3 300.	Initial tax credit of EUR 1 250, gradually declining to 0 by income of EUR 34 000.
Universal social charge	1.5% on first EUR 12 012, 3.5% on remainder to EUR 17 576, 7% thereafter to EUR 70 224 and 8% thereafter. Exempt if income below EUR 12 012.	0.5% on first EUR 17 000, 1% on remainder to EUR 27 000, 6% thereafter to EUR 39 000, 7% thereafter to EUR 70224 and 8% thereafter. Exempt if income below EUR 12 012.
Pay-related social insurance employee	4% of gross earnings. Exempt if income below EUR 18 304.	0.5% on first EUR 17 000, 4% on remainder. Exempt if income below EUR 12 012.

Source: Revenue Commissioners, Ireland.

2012). However, its design means that families with children may still find themselves in a low-income trap. The effective withdrawal rate (that is, the part of the marginal effective tax rate due to the withdrawal of benefits as income rises) for the low family income supplement is high at around 60% creating an overall marginal effective tax rate of 60-70% between 50 to 100% of the average wage (approximately EUR 16 000 to 32 000 per annum) (Figure 1.12).

To reduce the disincentive to work more for households with children, the government should redesign the low family income support supplement so that it falls more slowly with income. A possible benchmark is that it never exceeds the top marginal tax rate faced by high income earners. Simulation work using the ESRI SWITCH model suggests that reducing the FIS withdrawal rate from 60 to 32% and increasing the FIS income limits from EUR 602 to EUR 865 for a family with two children could raise disposable income in deciles 1 to 6, in some deciles by around 1 percentage points. This is estimated to cost approximately EUR 200 million (0.1% of GDP) at current take-up rates of 33%. If the take-up rate increased to 100%, the reform would cost approximately EUR 700 million (0.4% of GDP). It should also be acknowledged that, while this reform would lower METRs for the low paid, it would create higher METRs of those further up the income distribution (Table 1.5, O'Connor et al., 2015). However, this would bring the pattern more in line with the basic progressive nature of the Irish income tax system where METRs increase with income. A reform of the FIS payments should also try to reduce the large spike in the METR around 112% of the average due to the sudden withdrawal of the last EUR 1 040 of the FIS payment at that wage level. This could be done with two or more smaller steps down. A completely smooth withdrawal and METR would likely be too expensive.

Figure 1.12. **Lower income households with children face additional disincentives to work**

Total marginal effective tax rates 2015: Single earner couple, two children

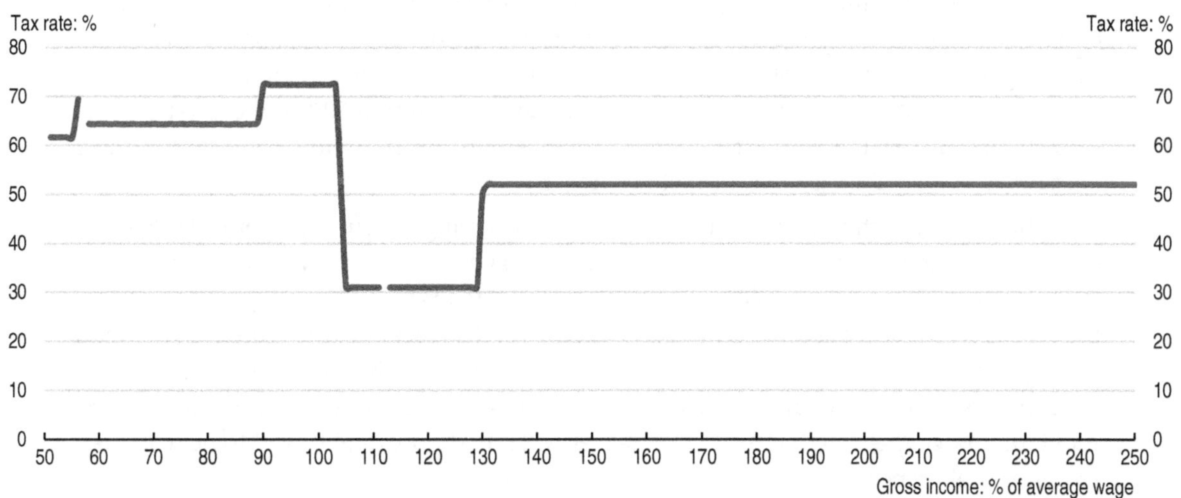

Note: The marginal tax rate is 154% at 57% of the average wage when PRSI becomes payable and 321% when the remaining EUR 1040 family income payment is removed at 112% of average wages. The tax rates include the combined effect of benefit withdrawal, income taxes, employee social security contributions and the universal social charge.

Source: OECD *Tax Wages Database*.

StatLink http://dx.doi.org/10.1787/888933275281

Table 1.5. **The marginal effective tax rate for the low paid can be reduced by changing in-work benefits**

Family Income Supplement – Distribution of change in marginal effective tax rates

Number of people in population ('000s) at base policy by change in METR

Original METR	Change in METR			
	≤ -20	> -20, ≤ -10	> 10, ≤ 20	> > 20
< = 20	0.00	0.00	0.00	**
> 20, < = 30	0.00	0.00	**	**
> 30, < = 40	0.00	0.00	16.86	10.77
> 40, < = 50	0.00	0.00	**	**
> 50, < = 60	0.00	0.00	**	0.00
> 60, < = 70	11.88	**	0.00	0.00
> 70, < = 80	**	**	0.00	0.00
> 80, < = 90	**	12.42	0.00	0.00
> 90, < = 100	0.00	**	0.00	0.00
> 100	**	0.00	0.00	0.00
Total	20.41	17.47	19.92	22.71

Note: Not all taxpayers shown. Most (1.7 million out 1.8 million) see practically no change in their METR (i.e. it is between -0.5 and 0.5% different. 34 000 taxpayers experience a shift of between -10 and 10% in their METR. Data for cells with low entries have been removed for data confidentiality reasons.

Source: O'Connor et al. (2015).

How to read this table: Due to the reduced withdrawal rates in the reform 11 880 people with a marginal effective tax rates between 60% and 70% experienced a reduction in their METR of more than 20%.

Raising revenue more efficiently: Personal capital taxes

Personal capital income tax rates in Ireland have been increased significantly post-crisis. The tax rate on interest in deposit accounts has increased from 20% in 2008 to 41% in 2015 and capital gains tax from 20% in 2008 to 33% in 2015. Taking a medium-term perspective and assuming a nominal rate of return of 4% and an inflation rate of 2%, the current rates of income taxes imply high tax rates on real returns. For taxpayers facing the marginal income tax rate of 40%, which would account for most of those with capital income of any note, the tax rate on real income returns is around 80% and capital gains is 66% (Table 1.6), leaving very little room to increase further marginal nominal tax rates without causing real after tax returns to go negative.

The main exception to these high real rates is investing in your own home. For owner-occupied housing, imputed rental income and capital gains, are exempt from tax, leaving the recurrent property tax, which is equivalent to real tax rate of 9% on capital income for properties worth less than EUR 1 million. One way to decrease the investment bias would be to increase the recurrent property tax further (discussed below). However, a higher property tax combined with income taxation on rents could result in negative real returns for landlords, suggesting that further increases to property tax might need to be restricted to non-rental properties.

Although there is little headroom to increase other capital income marginal tax rates, there seems to be scope to broaden the base for taxation of capital income. Reducing capital income related exemptions would mainly affect the very highest income bracket as around 60% of capital income goes to the top 10% of tax payers, and 30% to the top 1% of tax payers (Kennedy et al., 2015). The Superannuation related exemptions are costly. They have been reduced in recent years but they could be reduced further, especially given tax incentives on savings instruments tend to cause substitution from one instrument to

Table 1.6. **Taxation is not neutral across different asset classes**

Tax treatment of asset classes 2015

Asset class	Income taxes	Wealth taxes	Effective tax rate on real return
Interest-bearing accounts	40%	0%	82%
Fixed interest securities (bills and bonds)	Interest payments subject to income tax rate 20% or 40%. Capital gains tax 33%.	0%	40% or 80% on interest payments. 66% on capital gains. 0% on both interest and capital gains on Irish government bonds.
Shares	Tax at income tax rate, 20% or 40%. 33% tax on capital gains.	0%	Dividends: 40% or 80%. Capital gains: 66%.
Owner-occupied housing	0% on imputed rent. Personal private residence exempt from capital gains tax.	Recurrent property tax of 0.18% of the value of a property up to EUR 1 million and 0.25% on the value above EUR 1 million.	9% on properties up to EUR 1 million and 13% on value of property over EUR 1 million.
Rental housing	Rental income at income tax rate of 20% or 40%. 33% tax on capital gains.	Recurrent property tax of 0.18% of the value of a property up to EUR 1 million and 0.25% on the value above EUR 1 million.	Rents: 49% or 89% on properties up EUR 1 million. Capital gains : 66%.
Private pension accounts	Tax relief on contributions between 15% and 40% of earnings up to a limit depending on age. Lump-sum at retirement up to EUR 200 000 exempt, from EUR 200 000-EUR 500 000, 20%, over EUR 500 000 marginal income tax rate, 20% or 40%. Cash income taxed at marginal income tax rate.	0.15% on value of assets.[1]	Wealth tax and income tax: 48% or 88%.[2]

1. The temporary pension fund stamp duty levy was introduced in 2011 at a rate of 0.6% on funded pension scheme/plan assets. The original 0.6% levy applied for 4 years from 2011 to 2014 and ended last year. An additional levy of 0.15% was introduced in 2014 and 2015. The 0.15% levy ends in 2015. Liability for payment of the levy rests with trustees of the funds,
2. These calculations assume a real rate of return before tax of 2% but the effective tax rates would be lower at higher before tax real rates of return. This calculation does not take account of the tax relief on pension contributions and exemptions from tax for lump-sums.

Source: Revenue Commissioners, Ireland and OECD calculations.

another rather than an increase in savings (Engen et al., 1996; Attanasio et al., 2004; Chetty et al., 2012). This would help to improve investment neutrality as well as raising revenue in a way that puts the largest share of the burden on the highest income brackets.

Property taxes

As discussed above taxation treatment of property income is more favourable than other sources of capital income in Ireland. This distorts investment decisions and all else equal this will lead to over-investment in property. The first best approach is the taxation of homeowner imputed rental income, with deductions of inputs necessary to produce home services, including interest, which makes it neutral with respect to other investments as well as in terms of financing (Denk, 2012). One way to do this is through recurrent property taxes, which can be thought of as a tax on the flow of housing services on the assumption that this flow is proportional to the value of the real estate. Recurrent property taxes are more growth friendly than labour taxes, and are preferable to property transactions taxes in that transactions taxes tend to reduce mobility.

Ireland recently reduced property related transaction taxes (stamp duty was reduced from 9% to 1% on the value of a property up to EUR 1 million and 2% on the value above) and imposed a recurrent property tax (the local property tax, LPT) from 2013. The LPT is imposed as percentage of the value of the property, which is preferable from an equity point of view than the previous flat rate tax charged in 2012 (OECD, 2013b). The LPT raises approximately 0.3% of GDP, which is low by international standards in 2013 (Figure 1.13).

The LPT tax appears to be relatively easy to administer. The compliance rate is estimated at 96% and no-compliance results in a charge being imposed on the property. It

Figure 1.13. **Taxes on property are low by international standards**

Percentage of GDP, 2013[1]

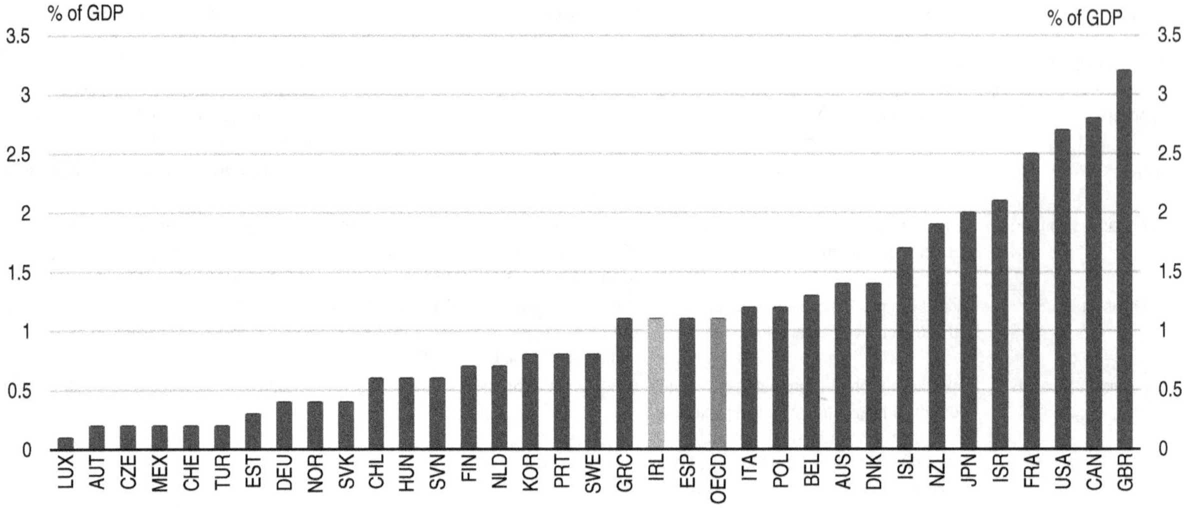

1. Or nearest year.

Source: OECD Revenue Statistics.

StatLink http://dx.doi.org/10.1787/888933275295

is imposed on self-assessed valuations based on guidance from the Revenue Commissioners, who can query and impose a valuation change if they consider the self-assessment is unjustified. Valuations are carried out every three years and in the absence of any policy changes the next valuation will likely see significant increase in LPT revenues. The LPT is currently levied on housing values at 1 May 2013. For the period 2017 to 2019 they will be based on valuations at 1 November 2016, which will likely be substantially higher given recent price movements. House prices have already risen between May 2013 and January 2015 by 12% and 38% outside Dublin and in Dublin respectively. The potential impact of home price increases on the LPT yield is currently the subject of an independent review.

From an inclusiveness point of view, the tax has some progressivity built into it, with a rate of 0.18% levied on all residential properties valued up to EUR 1 million and 0.25% imposed on any remainder of the value of the property exceeding EUR 1 million. However, the overall effect of the tax is moderately regressive, with the lowest deciles paying a higher percentage of their income in LPT (Keane et al., 2012; O'Connor et al., 2015). This is because housing ownership is quite high even in the lowest income quintile.

Simulations using the ESRI's tax-benefit model show that more revenue could be raised from the LPT, while also increasing its progressivity, by raising the LPT rate steadily with housing value and simultaneously granting a low-income waiver with marginal relief (O'Connor et al., 2015). The low income waiver would exempt those on modest incomes from the LPT entirely, which has the potential to create a poverty trap at the threshold. However, marginal relief limits the LPT liability to the minimum of the LPT liability or the difference between the waiver limit and the individual's income times the marginal relief rate. Marginal relief would ensure that individual's do not face an extremely high METR when they cross the low-income threshold.

Only a modest rise in the LPT rate may be needed to generate a substantial increase in revenues from 2017 given rapidly rising house prices. Regularly updating the valuations is important to maintain public acceptance that the tax is fair (Keane et al., 2012) and the LPT should remain directly linked to property values. However, given the sharp upward movement in house prices and the implied large step jump in LPT in 2017, consideration should be given to phasing in the increase in the LPT over more than one year.

Value added tax

Value-added tax (VAT) accounted for 27% of tax revenues in 2014. The standard VAT rate of 23% is high by OECD standards but the revenue base is relatively narrow (Figure 1.14) due to four reduced tax rates put in place to lessen the impact of VAT on the poor and promote social and cultural goals and support the tourism industry and employment. A rate of 0% applies to food and drink and children clothing, 4.8% rate applies to livestock including horses and greyhounds, and 13.5% applies to some fuels, building services, maintenance and cleaning and in 2011 this was reduced to 9% for tourism related services such as hotels and restaurants. Reducing labour taxes and raising more revenue from this source, especially by broadening the base, would improve the growth friendliness of the tax system and reduces distortions to consumption decisions induced by a multi-rate VAT system.

Reforms of this nature are opposed in Ireland, as elsewhere, on the grounds that raising either the standard or reduced VAT rates would be regressive. However, the tax expenditure from these reduced rates is substantial begging the question of whether these rates are efficient in achieving their distributional and other goals given the opportunity cost of significant revenue foregone. New micro-simulation analysis by the OECD of the distributional impact of reduced VAT rates in Ireland measured by the tax expenditure received by households in each income decile shows they are untargeted and are not an efficient way to assist the poor because the rich capture a large part of the benefits in

Figure 1.14. **The standard VAT rate is high but the revenue base is narrow**

VAT revenue ratio, 2011

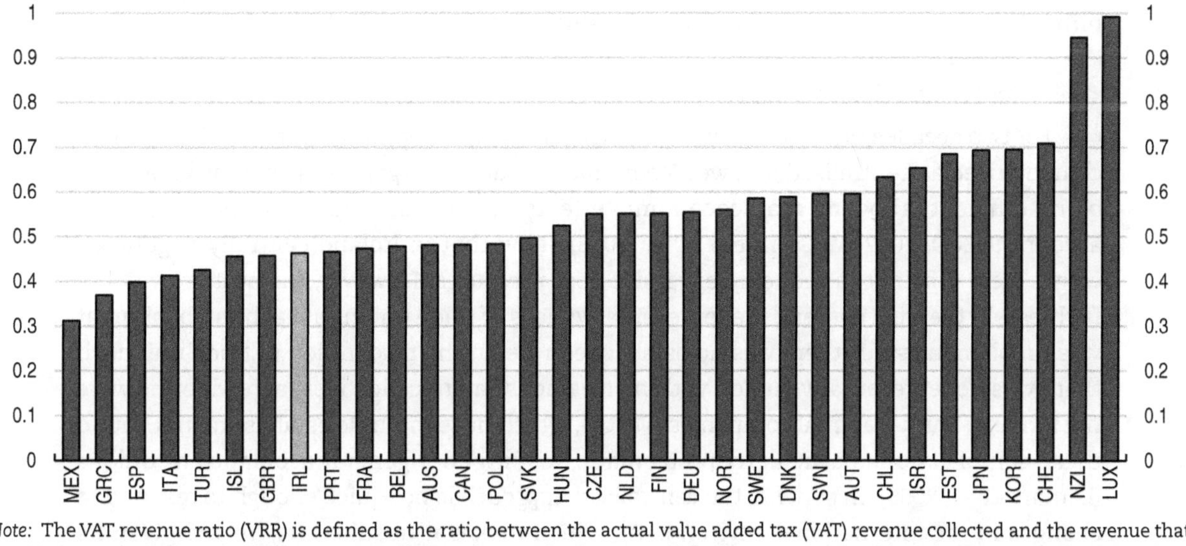

1
0.9
0.8
0.7
0.6
0.5
0.4
0.3
0.2
0.1
0

MEX GRC ESP ITA TUR ISL GBR IRL PRT FRA BEL AUS CAN POL SVK HUN CZE NLD FIN DEU NOR SWE DNK SVN AUT CHL ISR EST JPN KOR CHE NZL LUX

Note: The VAT revenue ratio (VRR) is defined as the ratio between the actual value added tax (VAT) revenue collected and the revenue that would theoretically be raised if VAT was applied at the standard rate to all final consumption. This ratio gives an indication of the efficiency of the VAT regime in a country compared to a standard norm. It is calculated as: VRR = VAT revenue/([consumption - VAT revenue] × standard VAT rate). Consumption is final consumption expenditure from the national accounts (heading P3).

Source: OECD (2014), *Consumption Tax Trends*.

StatLink http://dx.doi.org/10.1787/888933275302

absolute terms. The overall benefit from reduced rates for top income decile households is on average EUR 1759, while bottom income decile households benefit, on average, by only EUR 973 (Thomas, 2015). Overall it would be fiscally cheaper to eliminate the reduced rates and support the poor by transferring this latter sum to low income deciles via welfare and earned income tax credits, saving the tax expenditure currently enjoyed by higher income deciles.

Beyond efficiency there is also an issue of whether the rates are effective in improving the progressivity of the tax system. In Ireland reduced rates on food, pharmaceuticals, children's clothes and energy are progressive in the sense that the poor benefit more, in proportion to their income, from them than the rich (Thomas, 2015). However, others, particularly those on restaurant meals and accommodation, are regressive because high-income households spend far more on restaurants and hotels than low-income households (Thomas, 2015).

The low rates on accommodation and restaurants were partly in place with the goal of boosting employment in the labour-intensive tourism industry. Indeed reducing the rate on these services from 13.5% to 9% was an important measure of the government's *Jobs Initiative* policy in 2011 estimated to cost EUR 350 million. Whether or not this was effective is controversial. On the one hand, lower VAT rates appear to have been partially passed on in lower prices and employment appeared to grow faster in restaurant and accommodation and food services than the rest of the service sector following the introduction of the reduced rate (O'Connor, 2013). On the other hand, most of the growth in tourism numbers in 2011 occurred before the introduction of the rate reduction, changes in tourism market share in the UK and US markets appear to be correlated with other events and the price changes induced by the VAT rate change (around 2%) are small in comparison with exchange rate movements (Public Policy, 2013). They are also swamped by the general downward trend in accommodation prices induced by the crisis. Even if somewhat effective the recovery in the economy and labour market means the necessity of expensive measures such as the reduced 9% rate on tourism services should be reconsidered. Boosting low-skilled employment could be more effectively achieved by directly lowering hiring costs by reducing social charges or raising direct employment subsidies.

A more inclusive business sector

For two decades prior to the financial crisis, the wage bargaining system in Ireland was characterised as centralised and well-coordinated. Such a bargaining system is known for being efficient, allowing macroeconomic effects of wage settlement to be taken into account (OECD, 2012).McGuinness et al. (2008) show that in Ireland centrally negotiated wages were efficient in reducing excessive cost pressures. However, the system was not faultless. In the Irish context, the representativeness of trade unions at each establishment was problematic since there was no established rule on the recognition of trade unions: if there was no representative union within an establishment collectively agreed terms were not binding. Multi-national companies (MNCs), which have multiple establishments, found these complications particularly problematic, leading to a general avoidance of unions (Lamare et al., 2009). In general, the centralised approach is not quick enough to respond to changes in the international environment, which makes it unsuited for Ireland given its extremely high trade-to-GDP ratio. Ireland's centralised bargaining system broke down in late 2009 precisely because the largest business association refused to implement a wage agreement specifying an increase, which had been concluded in the previous year, at the height of the crisis.

Since the breakdown of the centralised bargaining system, wage negotiations take place at firm level. The firm-level negotiation system is known to be efficient in terms of flexible wage adjustments (OECD, 2012), as this enables firms to take into account firm-specific situations such as productivity. The swift labour cost adjustment following the crisis in Ireland was remarkable compared with other financially-constrained countries. The labour cost adjustment was likely facilitated by this wage setting framework, enabling the Irish economy to restore its competitiveness. Overall, the current wage setting system appears to be flexible enough to maintain cost competitiveness in the aggregate. However, wages negotiated at firm level are known to be more dispersed across different workers, which may aggravate income inequality. Indeed, returns to skills are likely to be more differentiated in the firm-level wage setting system (Dahl et al., 2011).

Lower income workers are partially protected by the minimum wage, which is the fourth highest in the OECD (hourly minimum wages after taxes in US dollars at purchasing power parities) for which data is available (OECD, 2015a). It was introduced in 2000 and its immediate effect was to raise the wage rate toward the lower end of the income distribution (Nolan et al., 2012). Although the minimum wage protects low-income workers, a balance must be struck; if it is set too high it will price low-skilled workers out of the job market.

The Low Pay Commission is tasked with making recommendations on the minimum wage. The Commission examines issues such as: the changes in earnings since the minimum wage was last increased in 2011; unemployment and employment rates generally; the expected impact of a change to the minimum wage on employment, the cost of living and national competitiveness; and changes in income distribution. It may also consider risks of a low-income trap, which would occur without coordination with other policies: high marginal effective tax rates at and just above the minimum wage level would restrain earnings prospects (OECD, 2015a).

Given the change in the bargaining regime to firm level, the business sector has a stronger role in delivering a high quality working environment and jobs. The broad parameters of how the business sector runs are determined by foundation governance arrangements. Such arrangements should create a business environment that encourages a more medium-term focus for business such as providing training and education relevant to the labour market and generating high quality jobs.

The *OECD Principles of Corporate Governance* (OECD, 2015b) help policymakers evaluate and improve the legal, regulatory, and institutional framework for corporate governance. Implementation of the Principles supports economic efficiency, sustainable growth and financial stability, helping to ensure the flow of external capital to companies both in the form of equity and credit. In Ireland, corporate governance standards are largely self-regulated and similar to those in the UK due to the similarities in accounting and legal systems. In addition, a body of Company Law regulates how companies should be structured, governed and managed (IBEC, 2010). Companies listed on the stock exchange either have to comply with its corporate governance requirements in the Stock Exchange (which include the provisions of the UK Combined Code) or have to explain the reason for non-compliance. Overall, the Irish corporate governance framework adheres to most of the OECD Principles and is considered to be well-performing, especially in terms of protection of investors, transparency of transactions and redress for violation of shareholders' rights.

As in other OECD countries, Ireland also faces a new challenge with the increasing influence of institutional investors, which the revised OECD Principles particularly deal with (OECD, 2015b). The share of equity investment held by institutional investors such as hedge funds and high frequency traders has increased significantly, with the direct relationship between the long-term performance of the company and the prosperity of the shareholder being broken (Isaksson and Celik, 2013). The growth of such intermediations has increased the potential for misaligned incentives and is likely to have encouraged economic short-termism (*The Kay Review*, 2012). Some countries have already introduced institutional investor codes to promote engagement in corporate governance and align institutional investors' interests with the ultimate beneficiaries (savers). The notable example of such codes is the UK Stewardship Code, which Ireland should consider following. The revised OECD Principles also recommend increasing disclosures for intermediaries, to ensure alignment of incentives and to take an active long-term interest in the companies.

Corporate governance is also concerned with finding ways to encourage the various stakeholders in the firm to undertake economically optimal levels of investment in firm-specific human and physical capital (OECD, 2015b). In Ireland, stakeholders' rights are laid down by case law: for instance, directors are required to have regard to the interest of the company's employees and members since the early 1990s (IBEC, 2010). However, it is not clear what the interest of the employees exactly means, for example, what it stands for in terms of investment in firm-specific human capital. Given the stronger role of firms in the bargaining process, the corporate governance framework should have a clear focus on encouraging investment in human capital. In turn, such arrangements would require that the corporate governance framework itself should be built on the performance of the company from a long-term perspective.

Multi-national companies (MNCs) in Ireland place much value on human capital. Their business model differs, but they commonly hire talented people and provide considerable amount of firm-specific training. Such training programmes are not necessarily limited to entry levels but generally provided over the course of career. Their emphasis on human capital is also reflected more broadly in terms of career development plans or job portfolio management. The enterprise value of MNCs in Ireland is generally very high, reflecting what they will be producing over the future, and high quality human capital seems to be an essential asset underpinning such valuations.

For smaller firms with fewer resources to invest, more collective approaches, including cooperating with large firms, would be appropriate. FIT, is a notable example of such an approach. FIT is an industry-led initiative, involving leading high-tech companies such as IBM. It's partly financed by the government and aims to act as bridge between the ICT industry and colleges, is a notable example of such approaches. FIT works also in close collaboration with government departments and national education and training agencies (including SOLAS and Education and Training Boards), local development organisations and a host of community based organisations. FIT identifies skill needs (according to which, there are more vacancies for people with skills at Level 5/6 on the National Framework of Qualifications than at the higher levels) and promotes technology-based programmes (apprenticeships) combining classroom training with workplace experience. The programmes develop not only ICT skills but also communication skills, project management, marketing and business acumen.

Box 1.1. **Corporate investment in human capital**

There is an opportunity to create a business environment that encourages a more medium-term focus for business and greater corporate sector involvement in broader societal challenges, such as providing training and education relevant to the labour market and generating high quality jobs. For individual firms, such involvement could be beneficial on its own, enabling them to enjoy better public relations and reputation among stakeholders, and ultimately benefiting the economy as a whole in which they operate.

Outreaching potential talents: Google's sponsorship in education programmes

Google sponsors a postgraduate certificate course in 21st Century Teaching and Learning launched at Trinity College Dublin. This programme aims to affect a significant long-term change in STEM education through a range of innovative interventions focused on the second level system. Google has provided funding of EUR 1.5 million to the College to support the programme. In this programme, 400 teachers are expected to take this certificate over the next three years. A further 600 teachers will have the option to take individual workshops or complete three course modules to earn a certificate of participation. Teachers participating in the programme will learn best practice in the use of technology in the classroom and consider related issues in respect of leadership and change management, inclusive education and school/classroom based research.

Google has also supported other programmes in the College, such as the Trinity Access Programmes (TAP) encouraging those who come from socio-economic groups under-represented in higher education; and Bridge 21 offering a new model of learning – team-based, technology mediated, project based and cross-curricular – which can be adapted for use in Irish secondary school.

Recommendations for increasing the inclusiveness of growth

Boost labour market participation and employment

- Continue to improve the evaluation of training and activation programmes. Scale-up those that are effective in helping people to return to the open labour market. Shut-down the ones that are not.
- Upskill long-term unemployed by improving both the quantity and the quality of training via public employment services or via private providers.
- Ensure that students receive information on educational options after schooling, notably vocational and technical options. Make available and publicise widely information on graduates labour market status and wages by degree and institutions, both for university graduates and for those that followed vocational and technical paths.

Improving mutual obligations

- Evaluate the effects of tightened conditionality in place since 2012 on the recipient's commitments to active job search and re-employment prospects.
- Fully enforce the obligations of the unemployed and improve the enforcement framework by defining more objectively the suitable offer that the benefit recipient has to accept in terms of wages and contract types.

Recommendations for increasing the inclusiveness of growth *(cont.)*

Improving the incentives to work by reducing welfare and income traps

- To reduce welfare traps, more gradually reduce housing assistance payments and family income supplement as income increases.
- To increase the incentive to work for the low-paid, smooth the increase in marginal effective tax rates by introducing a third income tax bracket and more gradually increasing universal social charge and pay-related social insurance rates.

Ensuring fiscal revenue and spending is more efficient and equitable

- Consider further reducing tax allowances for capital income from lump sum pension payments.
- Increase the local property tax rate and simultaneously introduce a low-income waiver to protect poorer households.
- Eliminate reduced VAT rates for restaurant meals and accommodation.

Wage setting

- Monitor regularly the effects of the minimum wage on employment patterns and adjust where necessary to ensure the low-skilled are not priced out of the labour market.
- Take into account the risk of a low-income trap when setting the minimum wage. Coordinate with other policies to avoid high marginal effective tax rates at and just above the minimum wage level.

Corporate governance

- Adopt institutional investor's codes to ensure alignment of incentives and to take an active long-term interest in the company.
- Together with social partners foster a strong business sector focus on building human capital through job training and career management.

Bibliography

AGTSW (Advisory Group on Tax and Social Welfare) (2012), "First Report: Child and Family Income Support", 27 March 2012.

Attanasio, O., J. Banks and M. Wakefield (2004), "Effectiveness of Tax Incentives to Boost (Retirement) Saving: Theoretical Motivation and Empirical Evidence", *IFS Working Papers*, W04/33, Institute for Fiscal Studies, *http://dx.medra.org/10.1920/wp.ifs.2004.0433.*

Auten, G., and G. Gee (2009) "Income Mobility in the United States: New Evidence from Income Tax Data", *National Tax Journal*, Vol. 62, No. 2.

Autor, D., F. Levy and R. Murnane (2003), "The Skill-Content of Recent Technological Change: An Empirical Exploration", *Quarterly Journal of Economics*, Vol.118, 1279-1333.

Bassanini, A. and T. Manfredi (2012), "Capital's Grabbing Hand? A Cross-country/Cross-industry Analysis of the Decline of the Labour Share", *OECD Social, Employment and Migration Working Paper*, No. 133, OECD Publishing, *http://dx.doi.org/10.1787/5k95zqsf4bxt-en.*

Bentolila, S. and G. Saint-Paul (2003), "Explaining Movements in the Labor Share", *Contributions to Macroeconomics*, Vol. 3, No. 1.

Bloom, N., M. Draca and J. van Reenen (2011), "Trade Induced Technical Change? The Impact of Chinese Imports on Innovation and Information Technology", *CEP Discussion Paper,* No. 1000.

Callan, T., N. Crilly, C. Keane, J.R. Walsh and Á. Ní Shúilleabháin (2011), "Tax, Welfare and Work Incentives" in *Budget Perspectives 2012*, Economic and Social Research Institute Ireland.

Central Statistics Office (2015), *Household Finance and Consumption Survey 2013.*

Chetty, R., J.N. Friedman, S. Leth-Petersen, T. Nielsen and T. Olsen (2012), "Active vs. Passive Decisions and Crowd out in Retirement Savings Accounts: Evidence from Denmark" , *NBER Working Papers*, No. 18565, National Bureau of Economic Research, *www.nber.org/papers/w18565.pdf*.

Dahl, C.M., D. le Maire and J.R. Munch (2011), "Wage Dispersion and Decentralization of Wage Bargaining", *IZA Discussion Paper* No. 6176, Bonn, November.

Denk, O. (2012), "Tax Reform in Norway: A Focus on Capital Taxation", *OECD Economics Department Working Papers*, No. 950, OECD Publishing, *http://dx.doi.org/10.1787/5k9bls0vpd5d-en*.

Denny, K. (2015), "The evaluation of the School Support Program under DEIS": An assessment". UCD Geary Institute for Public Policy, *Policy Peer Reviews series*, Geary PPR2015.02.

Department of Social Protection, *National Action Plan for Social Inclusion 2007-2016*, Dublin.

Engen, E.M., W.G. Gale and J.K. Scholz (1996), "The Illusory Effects of Saving Incentives on Saving", *Journal of Economic Perspectives*, Vol. 10, No. 4, American Economic Association.

Eurostat (2014), *Survey on ICT Usage and Ecommerce*.

González Pandiella, A. (2013), "Getting Irish Youth on the Job Track", OECD *Economics Department Working Papers*, No. 1101, OECD Publishing, *http://dx.doi.org/10.1787/5k3twr9k6s7h-en*.

Hijzen, A. and P. Swaim (2010), "Offshoring, Labour Market Institutions and the Elasticity of Labour Demand", *European Economic Review*, Vol. 54, No. 8, pp. 1016-1034.

IBEC (2010), *Corporate restructuring guidelines: Corporate governance*, Irish Business and Employers Confederation.

Isaksson, M. and S. Çelik (2013), "Who Cares? Corporate Governance in Today's Equity Markets", *OECD Corporate Governance Working Papers*, No. 8, OECD Publishing, *http://dx.doi.org/10.1787/5k47zw5kdnmp-en*.

Johansson, Å. et al. (2008), "Taxation and Economic Growth", *OECD Economics Department Working Papers*, No. 620, OECD Publishing, *http://dx.doi.org/10.1787/241216205486*.

Kay Review (2012), *The Kay Review of UK Equity Markets and Long-term Decision Making*, Department for Business, Innovation & Skills, London, *www.bis.gov.uk/assets/biscore/business-law/docs/k/12-917-kay-review-of-equity-markets-finalreport.pdf*.

Keane, C. (2012), "To Study or to Work? The Impact of a Construction Boom on Male Educational Attainment". Ph.D. Thesis Chapter. University College Dublin: Ireland.

Keane, C. (2014), "Gender Impact of Tax and Benefit Changes: A Microsimulation Approach", *ESRI Working Paper*, Economic and Social Research Institute, Ireland.

Keane, C., J.R. Walsh, T. Callan, M. Savage (2012), "Property Taxes in Ireland: Key Choices", *ESRI Renewal Series*, Paper 11, Economic and Social Research Institute, Ireland.

Kelly, E., S. McGuinness, P. O'Connell, A. González Pandiella and D. Haugh (2015), "How Well Does Ireland Integrate Migrants into its Labour Market?", *OECD Economics Department Working Papers*, forthcoming.

Kennedy, S., Y. Jin and D. Haugh (2015), "Taxes, Income and Economic Mobility in Ireland: New Evidence from Tax Records Data", *OECD Economics Department Working Papers*, forthcoming.

Lamare, J.R., P. Gunnigle, P. Marginson and G. Murray (2009), "Multinationals' Union Avoidance Practices at New Sites: Transatlantic Variations", Paper for MNCs Symposium, IIRA World Congress, Sydney, August.

McGuinness, S., E. Kelly, and P. O'Connell (2008), "The Impact of Wage Bargaining Regime on Firm-Level Competitiveness and Wage Inequality: The Case of Ireland", *ESRI Working Paper*, No. 266, Economic and Social Research Institute, Ireland.

McGuinness, S., P. O'Connell, and E. Kelly (2014), "The Impact of Training Programme Type and Duration on the Employment Chances of the Unemployed in Ireland", *The Economic and Social Review*, 45, Autumn 2014, 425-450.

Maître, B., H. Russell and C.T. Whelan (2014), "Trends in Economic Stress and the Great Recession in Ireland", *Department of Social Protection Social Inclusion Technical Paper*, No. 5.

Nolan, B., B. Maître, S. Voitchovsky and C.T. Whelan (2012), "Inequality and Poverty in Boom and Bust: Ireland as a Case Study", *AIAS Gini Discussion Paper*.

O'Connell, P. (2015), "The 2013 Follow-Up Survey of Former FÁS Trainees": An Assessment". UCD Geary Institute for Public Policy, *Policy Peer Reviews series*, Geary PPR2015.02.

O'Connor, B. T. Hynes and D. Haugh (2015), "The Distributional Consequences of Growth and Employment Enhancing Tax and Welfare Changes in Ireland", *OECD Economics Department Working Papers*, forthcoming.

OECD (2007), *OECD Employment Outlook 2007*, OECD Publishing, Paris, *http://dx.doi.org/10.1787/empl_outlook-2007-en*.

OECD (2011), *OECD Economic Survey of Ireland*, OECD Publishing, Paris, *http://dx.doi.org/10.1787/eco_surveys-irl-2011-en*.

OECD (2012), *OECD Employment Outlook 2012*, OECD Publishing, Paris, doi: *http://dx.doi.org/10.1787/empl_outlook-2012-en*.

OECD (2013a), *OECD Employment Outlook 2013*, OECD Publishing, Paris, *http://dx.doi.org/10.1787/empl_outlook-2013-en*.

OECD (2013b), *OECD Economic Survey of Ireland*, OECD Publishing, Paris, *http://dx.doi.org/10.1787/eco_surveys-irl-2013-en*.

OECD (2014), *OECD Science, Technology and Industry Outlook 2014*, OECD Publishing, Paris, *http://dx.doi.org/10.1787/sti_outlook-2014-en*.

OECD (2015a), *OECD Employment Outlook 2015*, OECD Publishing, Paris, *http://dx.doi.org/10.1787/empl_outlook-2015-en*.

OECD (2015b), *OECD Principles of Corporate Governance*, OECD Publishing, Paris.

O'Connor, B. (2013), "Measuring the Impact of the Jobs Initiative: Was the VAT reduction passed on and were jobs created?", *Administration*, 60, pp 161-179,

O'Connor, B., T. Heynes and D. Haugh (2015), "The Distributional Consequences of Growth and Employment Enhancing Tax and Welfare Changes in Ireland", *OECD Economics Department Working Papers*, forthcoming.

Public Policy (2013), Budget 2014: The Reduced Rate of VAT available at: *www.publicpolicy.ie/budget-2014-9-rate-vat/*.

Savage, M., T. Callan, C. Keane, E. Kelly and J.R. Walsh (2014), "Welfare Targeting and Work Incentives", *Budget Perspectives 2015 Paper 3*, Economic and Social Research Institute Ireland.

Savage, M., B. Colgan, T. Callan and J.R.Walsh (2015), "Making Work Pay More: Recent Initiatives", *Budget Perspectives 2016 Paper 2*, Economic Social Research Institute Ireland.

Thomas, A. (2015), "OECD Consumption Tax Micro-Simulation Model Results", Centre for Tax Policy, OECD, Paris.

Voitchovsky, S., B. Maître and B. Nolan, "Wage Inequality in Ireland's Celtic Tiger Boom", *Economic and Social Review*, Vol. 43., No. 1, Spring 2012, pp. 99-133.

© OECD 2015

Chapter 2

Migration in Ireland: Challenges, opportunities and policies

The Irish labour market is exceptionally open to international migration flows, thus making labour supply highly responsive to changes in cyclical conditions. Immigration also provides the skills that the Irish economy needs.. Prior to the recession, it provided labour for the construction sector. The crisis triggered a sharp reversal in migration flows, with immigration suddenly halting and emigration increasing. A large proportion of emigration is highly qualified, as is a high proportion of immigration. This pattern of "brain exchange" can contribute to reducing skills skills mismatches, but also raises the challenge of remaining attractive for skilled workers. This chapter examines how the crisis has affected migration, how related policies have evolved and proposes avenues to spread the benefits of migration beyond the scope of multinational enterprises, in particular to Irish SMEs. The proportion of Irish-born population living abroad is very large and the chapter also analyses what role return migration could play, what policies are in place to maintain links with emigrant's communities abroad and how they can be strengthened. Ireland has recently experienced, for the first time in its history, large-scale immigration. As a result, it currently hosts a large and very heterogeneous immigrant community, with diverging challenges and needs. Getting integration policies right is therefore a complex, but crucial task. The chapter identifies what are the key challenges in this area and proposes some avenues to foster the labour market integration of immigrants. Ireland is also starting to experience challenges associated with the integration of second generation immigrants. To respond to those challenges, the chapter recommends early action in education and social domains.

The Irish labour market is exceptionally open, with large migratory flows relative to the size of the labour force (Figure 2.1, panel A). Ireland has the highest share of nationals living abroad in the OECD (Figure 2.1, panel B): more than 17% of Irish-born persons aged 15 and over lives overseas. The share of foreign-born persons living in Ireland is also very high, reaching 20% of the total population, following a sharp increase over the years 2001 to 2011 (Figure 2.1, panel C). Foreign workers typically originate from other EU member states, as they benefit from free labour movement, as well as from other English-speaking countries.

The patterns of migration

Ireland exemplifies how rapidly migration patterns may change. For most of its history Ireland has been a country of emigration. This changed in the mid-1990s when the economic boom during the Celtic Tiger years slowed emigration and brought a substantial pick-up in immigration. Inflows of workers also increased strongly in 2005 when Ireland was one of the first countries to open its labour market to nationals from the Central and Eastern European countries acceding to the European Union (EU NMS). The latest recession caused a new turn in migration flows. Emigration resurged strongly, initially driven by nationals from EU NMS countries (Figure 2.2, panel A and C), followed as of 2010 by Irish nationals. The resulting population outflow has been large, both by international and Irish historical standards. More recent data show that emigration remains high, although the outflow of Irish and EU NMS countries nationals may have started to recede (Figure 2.2, panel C). Conversely, the emigration by nationals from other EU countries continues to increase. The recession also caused immigration flows to fall sharply in 2009, with a very gradual increase afterwards triggered by workers from non-EU countries.

These migration estimates are compiled by Ireland's statistical office based on movements in other migration indicators such as the number of Personal Public Service (PPS) identifiers allocated to non-Irish nationals, and the number of visas issued to Irish nationals to a number of destinations including Australia, United States and Canada. Data on national insurance numbers issued to Irish nationals in the United Kingdom is also used. Migration flows occurring through other channels and not registered in those indicators will not be captured in migration estimates. As a result, migration estimates tend to be subject to large uncertainty, in particular emigration estimates.

Countries of destination and origin have changed

The latest migration wave differs from previous migration episodes in terms of countries of origin and destination, as well as in terms of age and economic status of the migrants. An important shift in destination countries has taken place. The United Kingdom was historically the main destination country, receiving around 70% of all emigrants. The United States and Europe were the other main destinations. Although the United Kingdom remains a key destination country, now nearly half of the emigrants move to other countries, especially Australia and Canada. Countries of origin have also changed

Figure 2.1. **The Irish labour market is exceptionally open to migration flows**

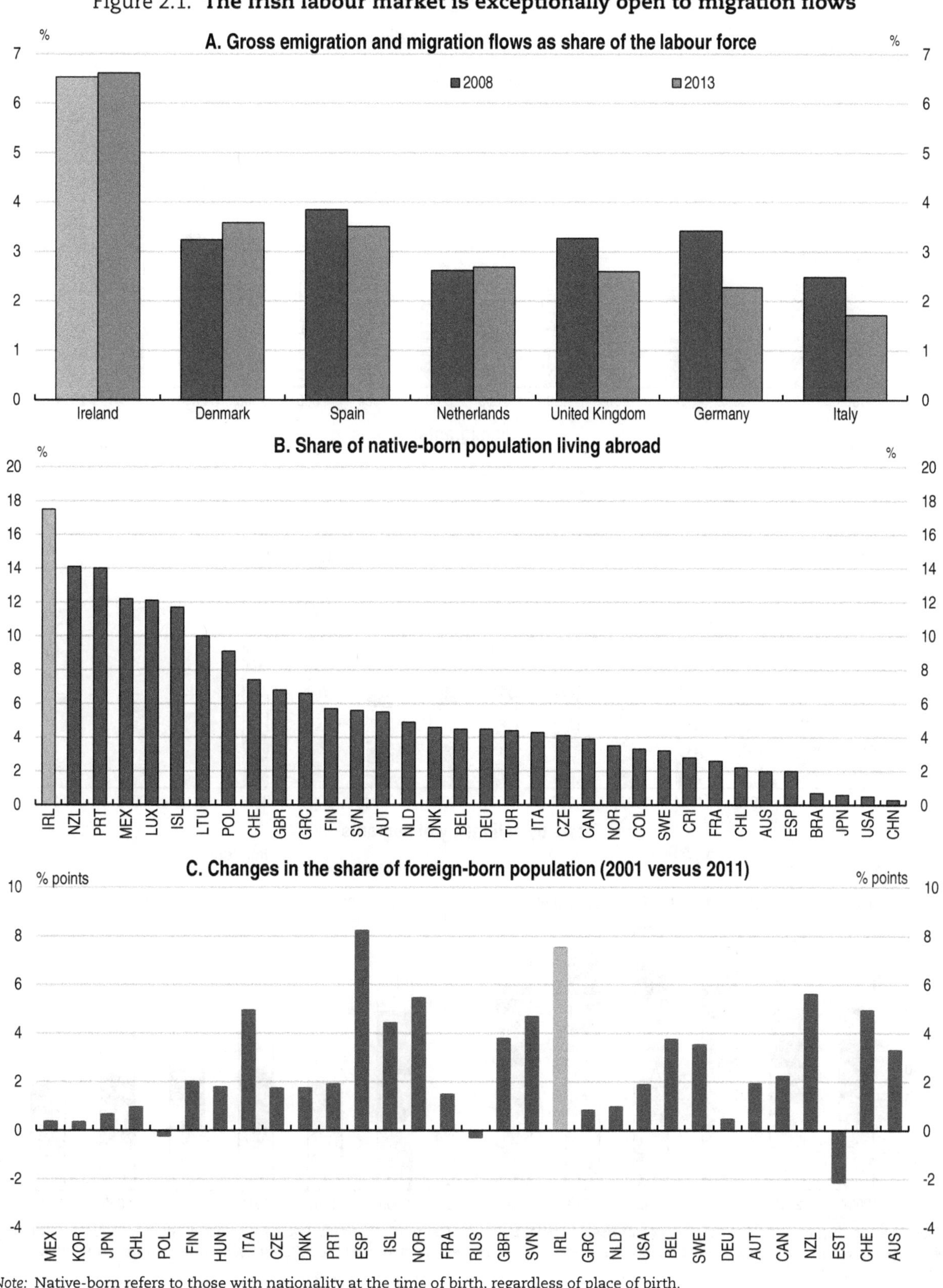

Note: Native-born refers to those with nationality at the time of birth, regardless of place of birth.
Source: Eurostat; Arslan et al. (2014); OECD (2014a).

StatLink http://dx.doi.org/10.1787/888933275312

Figure 2.2. **Destinations and origins have changed over time**

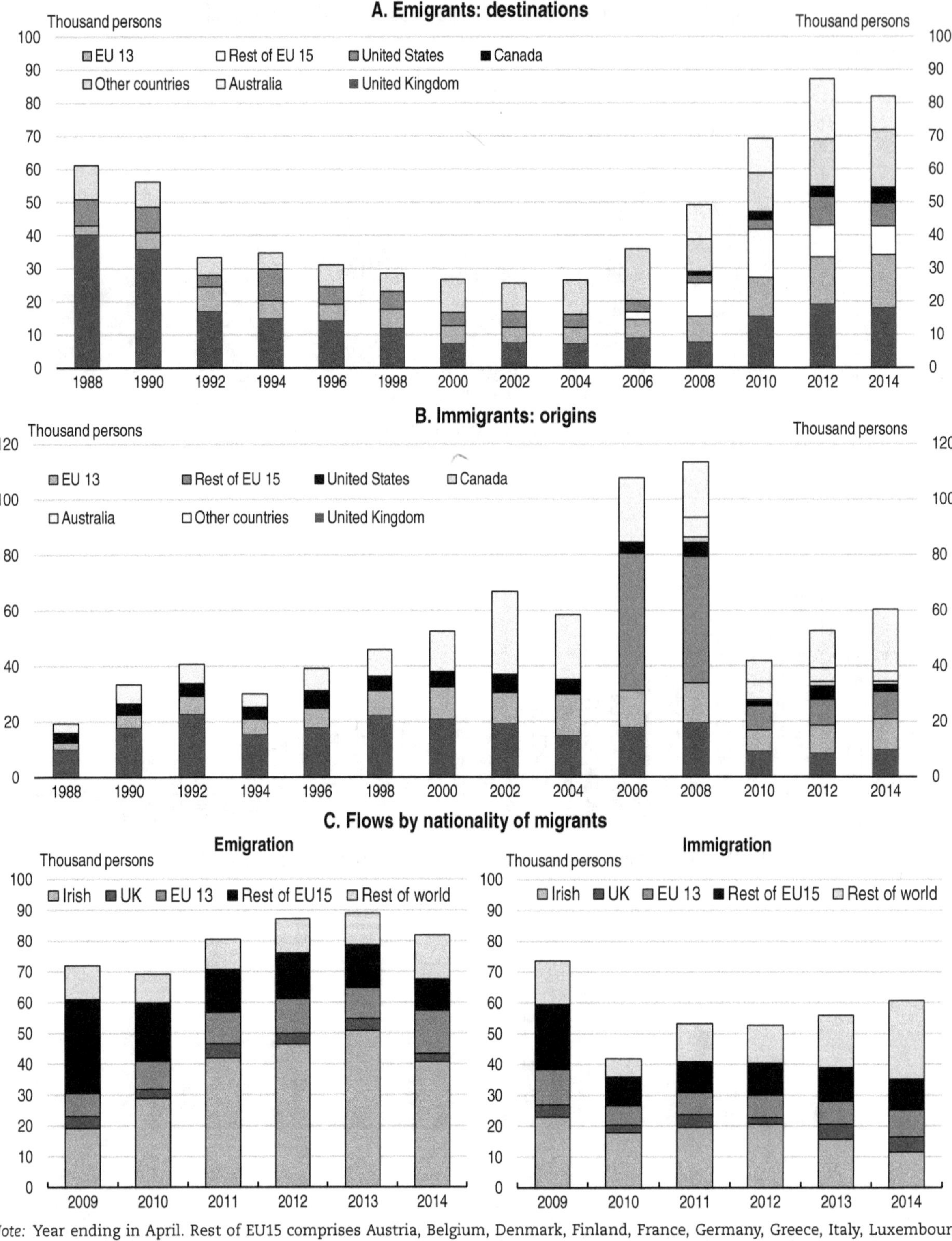

Note: Year ending in April. Rest of EU15 comprises Austria, Belgium, Denmark, Finland, France, Germany, Greece, Italy, Luxembourg, Netherlands, Spain, Sweden and Portugal. EU 13 include those countries that accessed the EU after 2004. Other countries include Canada and Australia before 2008.

Source: Central Statistics Office (CSO).

StatLink http://dx.doi.org/10.1787/888933275325

over the recession. Prior to the recession, immigration from EU NMS had grown rapidly. Workers from those countries, who do not need work permits, tended to be concentrated in lower-skilled sectors of the economy, such as agriculture, other production industries, construction, and wholesale and retail trade. As economic growth stalled in 2008 and activity in those sectors contracted, immigration from those countries declined sharply. There was a 40% fall in emigration from EU NMS in 2009, compared with 2008 and this fall continued over recent years. By contrast the inflow of workers from other countries outside the EU, who are largely working in higher-skilled sectors that suffered less severely during the recession, has continued to increase. The pick-up in emigration levels to EU13 and15 destinations is likely to also reflect return migration of those who came to Ireland in previous years from those destinations.

Another important change concerns age. Previous emigration episodes were largely driven by individuals aged 15-24. Although emigration continued to be large in this age group, the latest emigration wave has been led by those in the 25-44 age bracket (Figure 2.3, panel A). Immigration is also concentrated in youngest cohorts (Figure 2.3, panel B). In net terms, via the migration channel, Ireland has been consistently losing population in the 15-24 and 25-44 age brackets. Prior to the recession, Ireland had one of the largest youth cohorts of the OECD. After the recession this age advantage has decreased (Figure 2.4), especially in the 15-24 age bracket. Demographic challenges are not as pressing as in other OECD, but the existing cushion has diminished. Ireland has lower labour market participation rates than other advanced economies (Chapter 1). Hence, Ireland should remain proactive in adapting its policies to its rapidly changing demographics.

Most emigrants from Ireland were either employed or studying prior to their departure (Figure 2.7, panel A). Around 60% of those who left in 2009 were in employment, while 16% were unemployed. This has broadly continued over time. More recent data shows that around 40% of the people emigrating were in employment prior to their departure. This suggests that the unemployment situation may not be the only driver of emigration, but that better job rewards in other countries may drive emigration decisions as well. Salary

Figure 2.3. **Migration is concentrated in youngest cohorts**

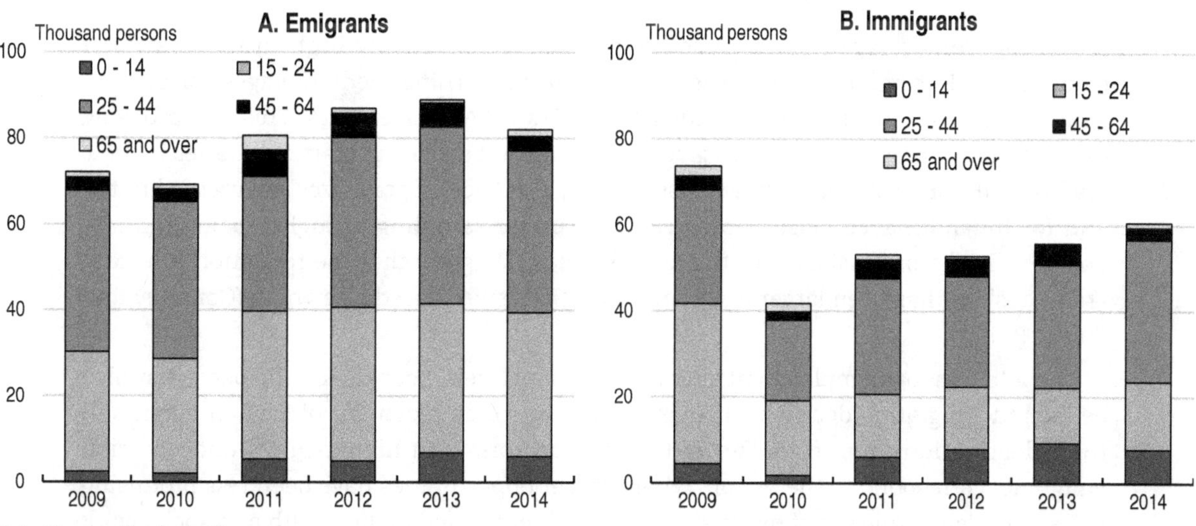

Note: Year ending in April.
Source: Central Statistics Office (CSO).

StatLink http://dx.doi.org/10.1787/888933275331

Figure 2.4. **The size of the Irish youth cohort has decreased**

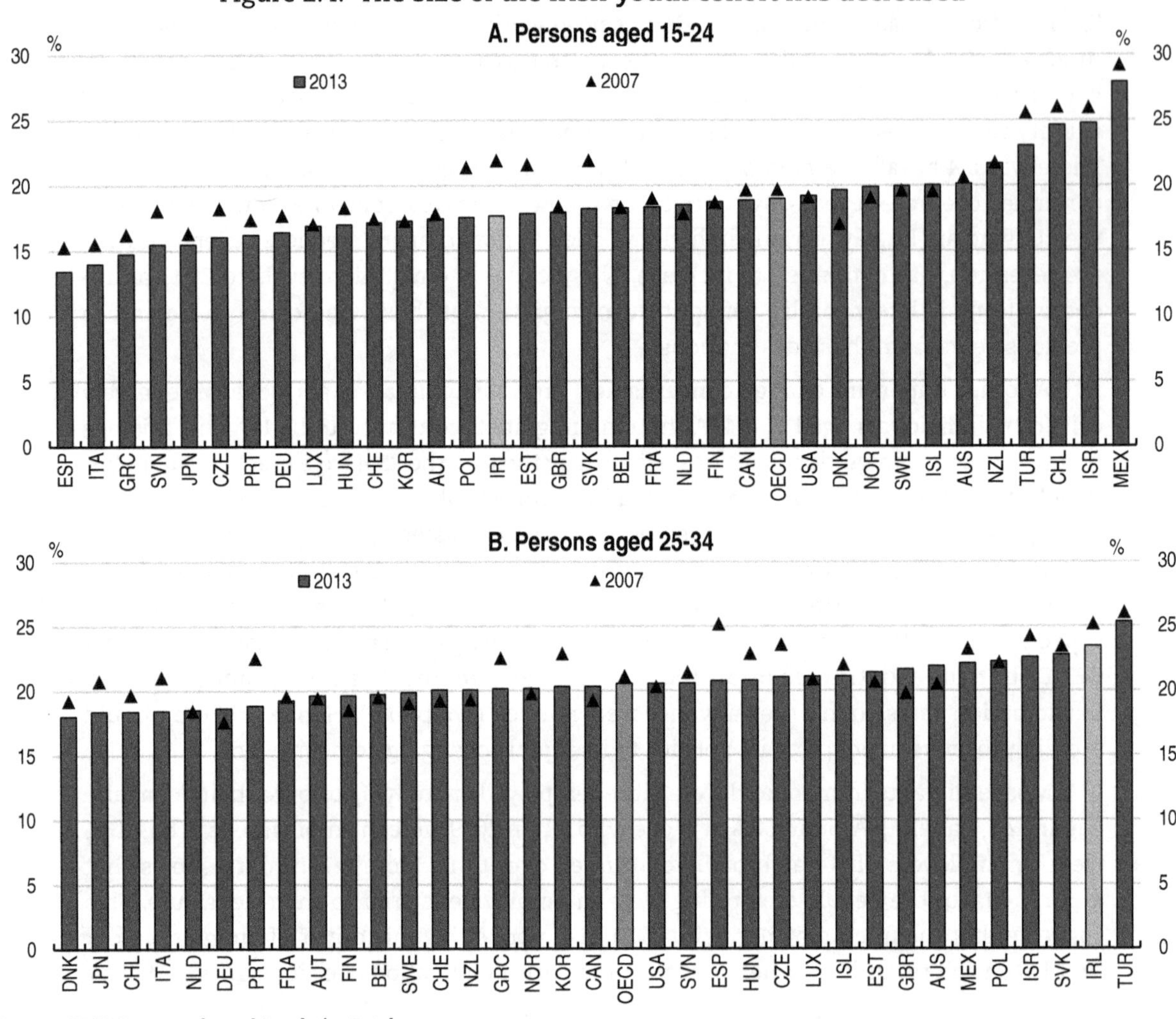

Source: *OECD Demography and Population Database.*

StatLink http://dx.doi.org/10.1787/888933275347

levels for workers aged 36 to 50 seem, on average, relatively high in international comparison. But Ireland seems less competitive concerning median wages for tertiary educated persons aged 20-30 according to OECD's PIAAC wages data. This has probably become more pronounced recently, given the significant decline in starting salaries for new graduates (Figure 2.5). Comparable cross-country evidence on graduates' salaries is limited and for Ireland maybe biased downwards by under-sampling of higher paid graduate positions in the professions, but the available data suggests that the reduction in recent graduates' pay has been larger in Ireland than that experienced elsewhere (Conefrey and Smith, 2014).

In addition to unemployment situation or salary levels, poor career prospects may also be behind emigration decisions. Looking at sectors of employment of Irish emigrants in their destinations countries shows that the sectors with higher prevalence of Irish emigrants correspond to the sectors where career opportunities have been less promising in Ireland. Hence, one out of five Irish emigrants is employed in the health and social work sectors in their destination countries (Figure 2.7). They are also significantly employed in the education sector. Career opportunities in these sectors in Ireland have been affected by

Figure 2.5. **Salaries for recent graduates have declined**

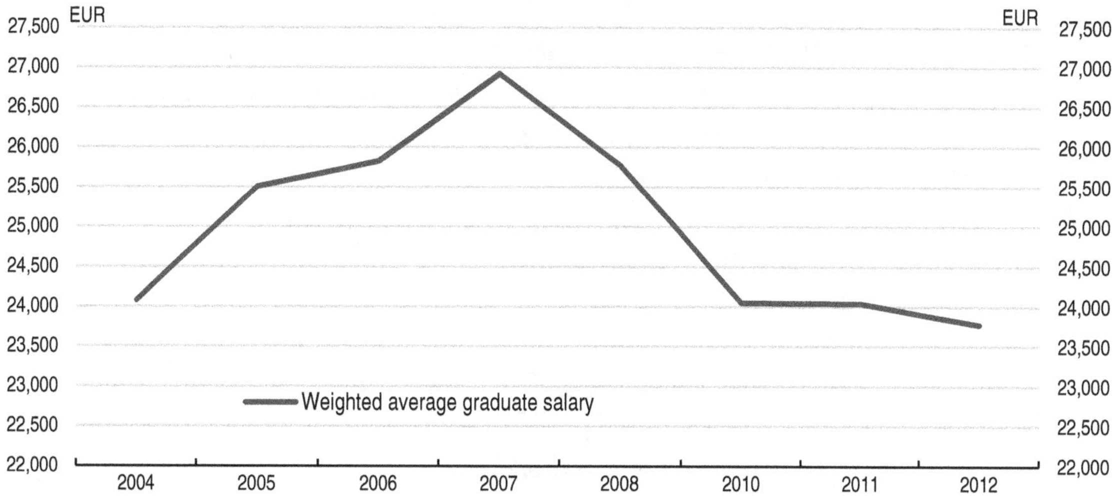

Source: Conefrey and Smith (2014).

StatLink http://dx.doi.org/10.1787/888933275357

the moratorium in public recruitment in place between March 2009 and October 2014. A significant proportion is also employed in real estate, renting and business services sector, which experienced a severe contraction during the recession.

On the immigration side, a substantial proportion of immigrants in Ireland are in employment (Figure 2.6, panel B). The proportion of those coming and staying unemployed has diminished over the recession. The share of immigrants who come to study has been relatively small, although it has increased recently, accounting for 16% all immigrants that came to Ireland in 2014.

Figure 2.6. **Many emigrants were in employment prior to their departure**

Persons aged 15 and over

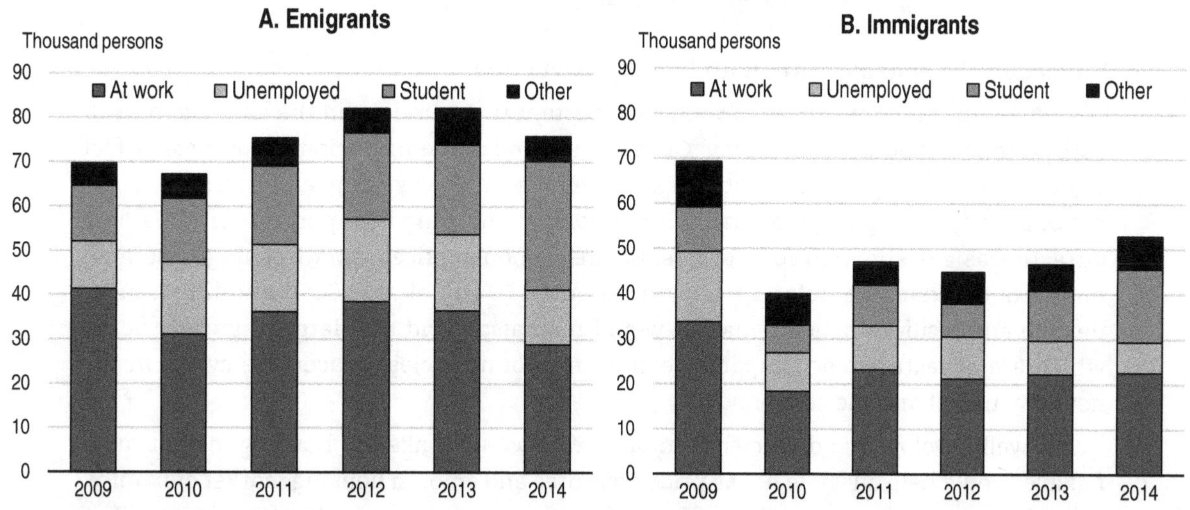

Note: Year ending in April.

1. As a person's principal economic status can change over the course of the year, for immigrants this refers to their status in the quarter prior to the April of the year in question, while for emigrants it is their status in the period prior to departure.

Source: Central Statistics Office (CSO).

StatLink http://dx.doi.org/10.1787/888933275364

Figure 2.7. **One out of five Irish emigrants is employed in the health and social work sector**

By education level

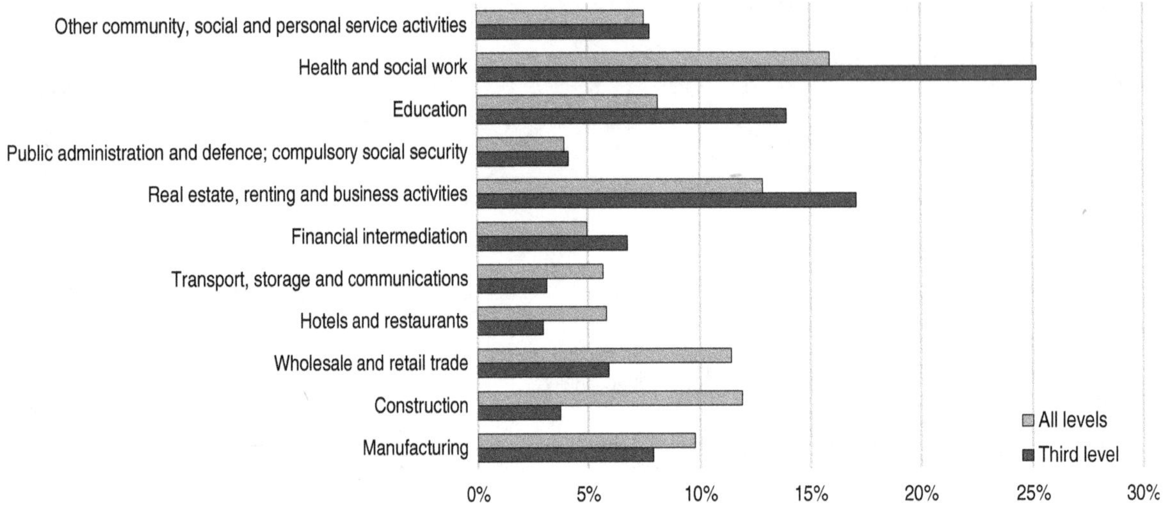

Other community, social and personal service activities
Health and social work
Education
Public administration and defence; compulsory social security
Real estate, renting and business activities
Financial intermediation
Transport, storage and communications
Hotels and restaurants
Wholesale and retail trade
Construction
Manufacturing

0% 5% 10% 15% 20% 25% 30%

All levels
Third level

Source: OECD DIOC 2010/11.

StatLink http://dx.doi.org/10.1787/888933275378

The economic impact of migration

Large migration flows have very wide economic implications and this chapter focuses its analysis on two particular economic aspects. First, it assesses the interaction of migration and the housing market and infrastructure. Large migration flows are likely to be a permanent feature of the Irish economy, so it is important to assess how the housing market can be made resilient to sudden changes in population, and what parts of the infrastructure are more likely to be affected. Secondly, it examines the impact that migration is having on the size and composition of the labour force. Emigration has played an important role in Ireland as a macroeconomic adjustment mechanism, preventing unemployment rates above 20% seen in other crisis countries and limiting scarring effects of being out of work. But it also entails trade-offs and risks.

Impact on the housing market and on infrastructure

Fluctuations in migration flows have important repercussions in the housing market, both in Ireland and internationally. On the one hand, large migration inflows can affect significantly house prices by putting extra pressure on the existing supply. On the other hand, a ready supply of good quality and affordable housing is important for remaining attractive as a destination for workers. Booms in house prices can discourage potential migrants and damage Ireland's growth potential (Duffy et al., 2005). Building a more flexible and resilient housing market would help also avoid that large migration flows, which are expected to accompany Ireland's economic cycles, exacerbate cycles in the housing market and the economy.

A well-developed and efficient rental market would make the housing market more flexible, would help alleviate house price pressures and smooth housing market dynamics. It would serve as a more suitable and affordable option than ownership for migrants. The Irish housing market is characterised by a high ownership rate. Rental contract legislation is perceived to be complex and difficult to understand (DKM, 2014). The quality in some segments of the rental market, especially apartments in Dublin, is poor. This pushes many, including recent migrants, into the ownership ladder. There are regulations setting standards for rented properties but their implementation varies. Stepping up efforts to check the compliance with existing quality standards would contribute to improving the quality of the rented stock.

The supply of rentals is at historically low levels. This is particularly so in Dublin, where there are also upside pressures on rents caused by high demand of apartments in some specific locations in the inner city area. More professionalised private rental markets and a greater emphasis on increasing density within the metropolitan areas, as envisaged in Construction 2020 government strategy, are thus welcome.

Migration flows can also have important repercussions for physical and social infrastructure. In the past, migration and the resulting rapid increases in population contributed to infrastructure bottlenecks. A significant proportion of migrants tend to live in commuters belts around the main city centres and traffic congestion problems were significant before the recession. With the return to robust economic growth, congestions and infrastructure bottlenecks will become apparent again, especially in the Dublin area. Urban and housing planning are now more focused on increasing density than they were in the past, which will help to increase the viability of public transport options as well as other sustainable transport options (Assessment and Recommendations).

Migratory flows can also add to pressures on social infrastructure, such as schools or health centres. Irish schools have experienced a rapid increase in the inflow of immigrant students, with a large proportion of students for whom English is not their first language, which creates additional needs, especially in disadvantaged schools (more below). In healthcare, immigration has not translated so far into significant additional demands in terms of volume, although the need to treat patients with differing cultural and linguistic backgrounds raises new challenges.

Impact on the labour force

The recession triggered a surge in emigration, less immigration and a fall in participation among Irish workers, all of which made the labour force shrink by 5% from 2008 to 2014. Despite the improvement in the economy, labour market participation rates are expected to remain fairly low (Central Bank of Ireland, 2015). Hence, migratory flows will play a key role in labour force dynamics. These dynamics will depend on how responsive migratory flows are to the on-going recovery in Ireland and other advanced economies. In countries with a high proportion of jobseekers, changes in unemployment rates tend to be a good proxy to gauge how economic opportunities evolve over time and affect migration flows (Izquierdo et al, 2015). Bilateral migration equations suggest that migration flows both from and to Ireland are significantly affected by the unemployment rate differential between the United Kingdom and Ireland (Annex). This link, although weaker than in the 1990s, remains significant, especially on the emigration side. Both outflows and inflows are also found to be responsive to unemployment rate differentials with the United States and the euro area, although to a lesser extent. The link with unemployment dynamics in other countries is weak on the emigration side, reflecting that emigration to countries such as Australia, Canada and New Zealand is heavily related to visa rules, which tend to be linked to skills needs in those jurisdictions. However, these host locations have not recently experienced a shock in unemployment rate dynamics of sufficient magnitude to test this relationship. Conversely, immigration from other countries to Ireland is found to be sensitive to unemployment differentials. This is largely driven by immigrants from EU NMS countries. A proportion of the workers that came from these countries during the boom years left when the crisis started and unemployment soared.

Forecasting migration flows is subject to significant uncertainty. Nevertheless, some indicative projections can be obtained using the elasticities from the bilateral migration equations and OECD forecasts for unemployment rates. These indicative projections provide an indication of how migration to and from Ireland is expected to evolve based on the expected macroeconomics developments in Ireland and in other economies. These projections suggest that migration outflows, while remaining significant, will continue a very gradual deceleration in the coming years in line with the overall improvement in the Irish economy (Figure 2.8). In the same vein, immigration will continue to progressively pick up. As a result net migration is expected to decrease but still stay negative over the period to 2016. Thus, its contribution to labour force growth would remain negative, although it will diminish and eventually become positive provided the improvement in Ireland's economy continues and strengthens. A return to its pre-crisis level seems more distant though, absent a large on-off factor such as further opening of the labour market to more EU countries as occurred in the early 2000s.

Migratory flows affect not only the quantity of the labour force but also its quality. Initiatives under the annual *Action Plan for Jobs* have expanded IT training places but these take time to bear fruit. Immigration has played a crucial complementary channel to extra training, providing the human capital that the multinationals sector requires, and that the local education and training system was unable to generate fast enough especially in the IT sector. The share of the foreign born population in Ireland that is highly educated is particularly large (Figure 2.9). More than 40% of foreign-born workers have a university degree. This compares with just over 30% amongst native born workers net of migration outflows.

Figure 2.8. **Net migration is expected to remain negative in the short run**

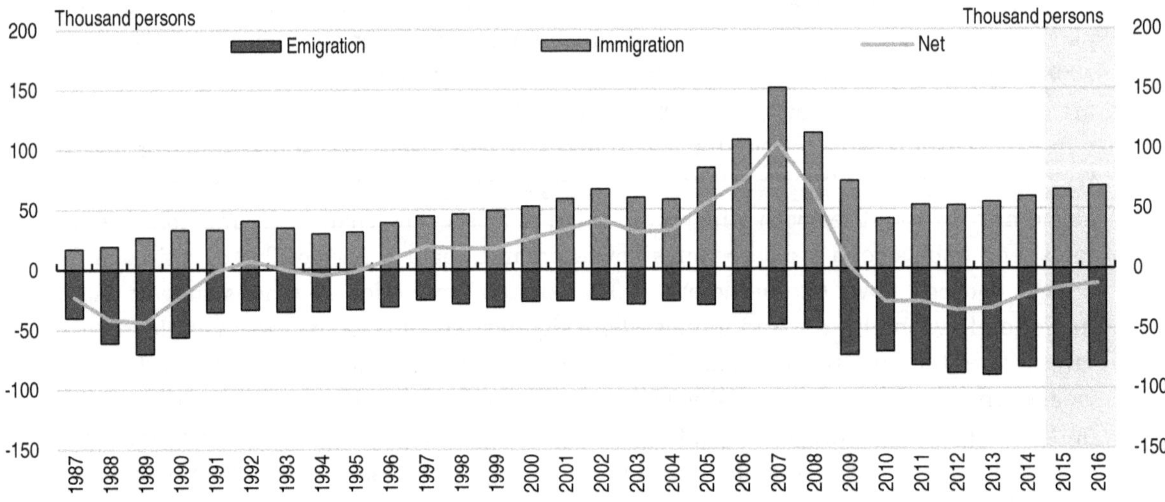

Source: CSO up to 2014. Projections for 2015 and 2016, based on equations described in Annex and unemployment rates as projected in *OECD Economic Outlook 96*.

StatLink http://dx.doi.org/10.1787/888933275382

Figure 2.9. **The share of the foreign born population that is well-educated is high**

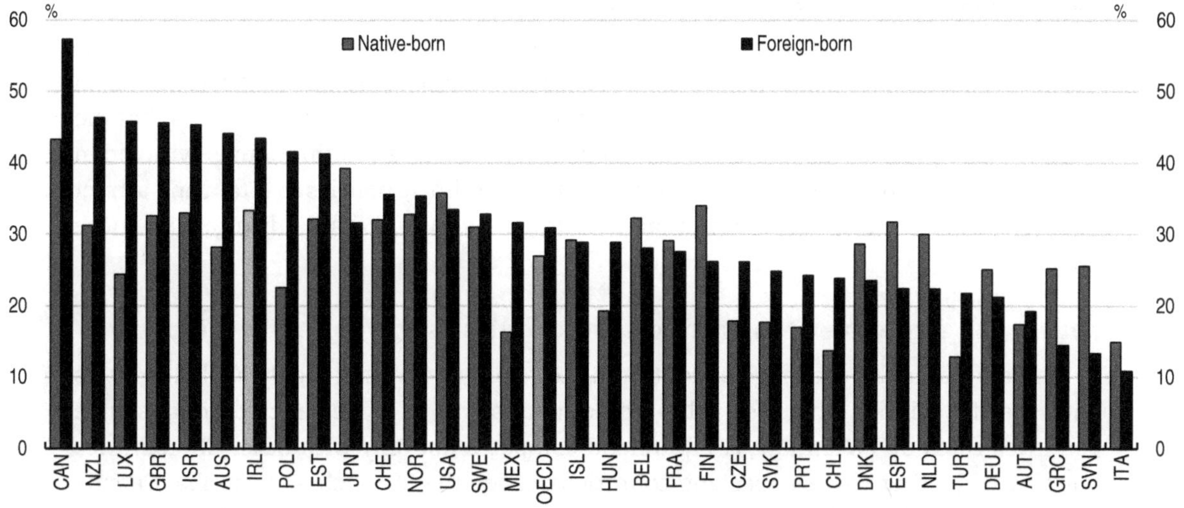

Source: OECD International Migration Outlook 2014.

StatLink http://dx.doi.org/10.1787/888933275394

Overall, Ireland has been exhibiting a pattern of "brain exchange", whereby highly educated workers flow from and to Ireland. Even during the recession, despite its depth and severity, the inflow of highly educated workers continued (Figure 2.10, panel B). At the same time, a significant proportion of emigration corresponded to individuals with tertiary qualifications (Figure 2.10, panel A). More recent data shows that while total emigration has started to decline, emigration by individuals with tertiary education continues to increase. Thus, despite the general improvement in the Irish economy and its labour market, the outflow of university graduates continues to exceed the inflow. With lower

Figure 2.10. **Migration is large among highly educated individuals**

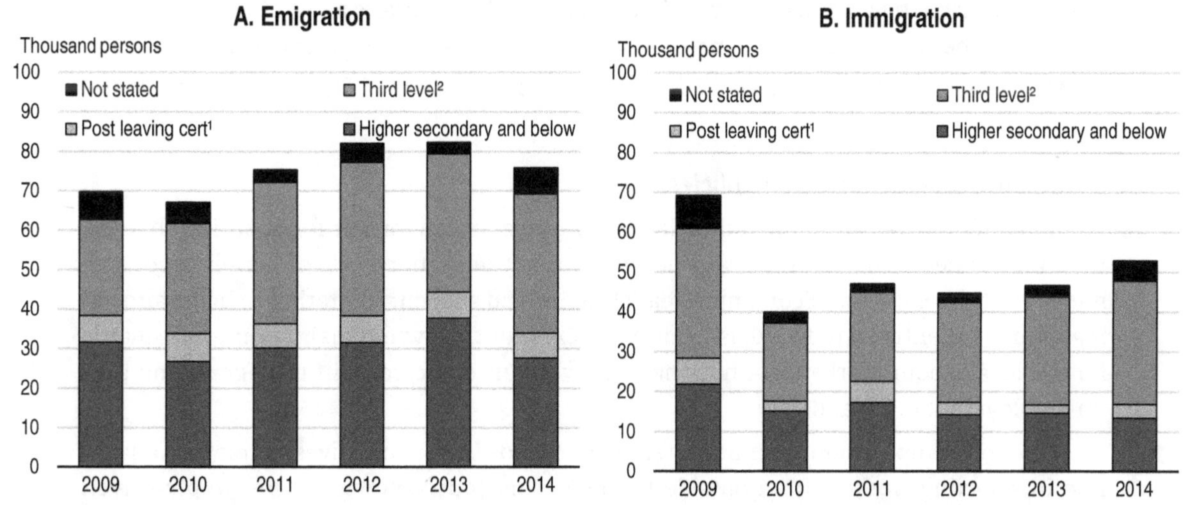

Note: Year ending in April.

1. Technical or vocational, advanced certificate or diploma.
2. Pass degree and above.

Source: Central Statistics Office (CSO).

StatLink http://dx.doi.org/10.1787/888933275402

post-crisis starting salaries (Conefrey and Smith, 2014), many of the young and educated may feel that prospects are brighter elsewhere.

Productivity prospects of domestic companies, whose ability to hire workers abroad is limited, are more likely to be affected by the outflow of domestic qualified workers than multinationals, which are more successful in international recruitment. This risks that the already large productivity gap between domestics firms and multinationals will widen even further; it also highlights the need for Ireland to optimise policies to retain and attract qualified workers, and to facilitate that all companies can take full advantage of these policies.

Maintaining the attractiveness of Ireland as a destination for skilled workers

Ireland faces the challenge of continuing to retain and attract highly skilled workers with specific abilities. That task will become more acute, as wages in traditional source countries catch up (Westmore, 2014). Ireland competes not only with other EU countries but also with other English-speaking countries outside the EU, such as Australia, Canada and New Zealand, which have specific migration programmes for skilled migrants, a solid track record as attractive destinations for migrants, and a proven ability to retain them (OECD, 2014c). Other countries, such as those of the Persian Gulf, Singapore, and China, have also started to attract highly-skilled personnel (Docquier and Marfouk, 2006) and aim at increasing further the attractiveness of their jurisdictions for skilful workers as a way to support a diversification of their economies.

Multinationals play a central role in attracting the skilled to Ireland. The proportion of immigration that takes place through the organisational channels of these transnational firms (e.g. intra-company transfers) is not particularly high but multinationals are the main employers of those being granted employment permits. The presence of IT multinationals, such as Google, IBM, Microsoft and Apple, in Dublin acts as a powerful magnet for workers, especially from Europe. While these firms contribute to cementing Ireland's reputation as a destination country for migrants, Ireland could do more to improve its attractiveness as a destination for high-skilled workers and to facilitate that all companies benefit from the openness of the labour market. This concerns migration policy, and also the availability of affordable housing and a good provision of education and health.

Optimising labour migration policies

Effective and efficient migrant selection policies are important for ensuring that the full range of necessary skills is available swiftly and transaction costs are minimised. As a member of the European Economic Area (EEA), Ireland's labour migration policies aims at regulating the entry of individuals from non-EEA countries while maintaining safeguards for the local labour market. EEA nationals enjoy an unrestricted right to migrate and take up employment in Ireland.

The Irish employment permit system is demand-driven, and gives employers a large role in selecting workers from outside the EEA. This contrasts with more supply-driven systems in countries that use point systems, whereby potential migrants are selected on the basis of criteria such as education, languages proficiency or previous working experience. Those surpassing those criteria can then enter the country and search for employment, although the number of people accessing those countries without a job offer has become quite small (OECD, 2014a). The existing employment – permit system seems a suitable approach for Ireland given that the system is intended to regulate only the entry of non-EEA workers, which is a limited proportion of total immigration. The system should continue to be adjusted to the changing nature of immigration and to ensure that it is achieving its objectives. Ireland has recently made a number of changes to employment – permits to facilitate access for qualified workers (Box 2.1).

The framework should continue to be monitored, in particular to ensure that the salary thresholds, which are relatively high in international perspective for occupations not included in the Highly Skilled Eligible Occupations List, do not act as a barrier for recent graduates, especially as wages for tertiary educated workers aged below 30 have fallen considerably. Establishing a differentiated salary threshold for younger workers may be needed. Another aspect to closely monitor is the friendliness of the system towards SMEs, which tend to have more difficulties in recruiting internationally than larger firms. In such cases, providing SMEs with specialised support in international recruitment processes, via Enterprise Ireland, could help them to attract internationally the skills they need and are unable to find in the local labour market.

Employment permits could be further simplified through so-called trust-based schemes, which have been recently launched in Ireland, the so-called Trusted Partner Initiative. Under this initiative, the employment permit application is replaced by the insertion of a Trusted Partner Registration Number and a confirmation that there have been no changes to the details already provided during their Trusted Partner registration. Thus, participating employers benefit from shorter permit processing times, fewer supporting documentation requirements, and a waiver of labour testing requirements.. This sort of programme, operated also in some other OECD countries, works under the presumption that employers have sufficient incentives to check themselves that their applicants meet all conditions. The scheme has potential to reduce administrative burdens significantly and to accelerate permits issuance. SMEs are more likely to have higher obstacles to benefit from these simplified schemes due to higher costs of meeting the requirements, as they do not have the advantages of larger firms to operate these schemes, such as human resources departments or economies of scale. In contrast to other countries, the registration as a Trusted Partner is free of charge in Ireland, which should facilitate SMEs participation. The authorities should monitor the scheme to ensure it continues to meet the needs of all enterprises including SMEs.

A swift and low-cost application process for employment permits is a key ingredient for an efficient migration policy. Significant progress has been made by Ireland in reducing processing times for employment permits. The average processing time was 74 days in 2010, but following changes to streamline the application process, the average wait time was reduced to 32 days in 2011 and to 18 days in 2014. This compares favourably with processing times in other OECD countries (OECD, 2014a). However, processing costs for permit issuance are high in international perspective (OECD, 2014a). High fees may not put employers off hiring needed highly skilled workers in significant demand, but might deter potential migrants. The principle underpinning the charging of fees for employment permits in Ireland is cost recovery, both processing and compliance costs. Making further use of IT in employment permits processes would deliver efficiency gains and savings, which should be passed on in lower fees. Ireland plans to upgrade the IT infrastructure underlying the application process, with the aim of setting up an online application facility that would include payment options. In the same vein, the swifter Trusted Partner

Box 2.1. **Employment permits in Ireland**

As of September 2014, Ireland's Employment Permit (EP) system comprise the following types of permits available to non-EEA nationals (DJEI, 2014):

- *Critical Skills EPs*. It replaced the Green Card permission and is targeted at highly demanded and skilled occupations that are in significant shortage of supply. It currently includes occupations such as ICT professionals, professional engineers and health professionals. A labour market test is not required and permit holders can apply for immediate family reunification. Critical skills permits are issued in respect of a job offer of 2 years' duration. Occupations should have a minimum annual remuneration of EUR 30 000 for the occupations contained in the so-called *Highly Skilled Eligible Occupations List* (see below), or EUR 60 000 otherwise.
- *Intra-Company Transfer EPs*. It is designed to facilitate the transfer of senior management, key personnel or trainees, who are non-EEA nationals, from an overseas branch of a multinational corporation to its Irish branch. The foreign employee must have worked for the foreign entity for at least 6 months.
- *General EPs*. Unlike Critical Skills EP, all occupations are eligible except those on the Ineligible Occupations List. Their issuance is contingent on a job offer from a bona fide employer. Minimum annual remuneration is generally EUR 30 000. It is EUR 27 000 for non-EEA students graduated in the last 12 months who have been offered a graduate position from the *Highly Skilled Eligible Occupations List*.
- *Dependent/Partner/Spousal (DPS) EPs*. It allows dependants, civil partners, and spouses of certain categories of EP holders to apply for an employment permit to work in Ireland.
- *Contract for Services EPs*. It caters to the situation where a foreign entity has won a contract for services at an entity in Ireland, and is sending non-EEA nationals to Ireland to carry out the contract.
- *Internship EPs*. It applies to students enrolled in a fulltime degree course or higher at an overseas institution, who take on an internship in Ireland as a mandatory part of their studies. It is issued with a maximum validity of one year, unrenewable, and the intern needs to return home to continue their study after completion of the internship.

Other existing EPs include *Reactivation EPs*, aimed at foreign nationals who entered the State on a valid Employment Permit but who fell out of the system, and *Sports and Cultural EPs*, for those going to work in the development, operation and capacity of sporting and cultural activities.

The *Highly Skilled Eligible Occupations List* is determined in line with the regular analyses of an *Expert Group on Future Skills Needs*. It is organised using the Standard Occupational Classification system (SOC 2010), an international system which classifies workers into occupational categories. Within these broad categories, specific capabilities or skills are also included in the list and should be met to become eligible for the Critical Skills EP. There is also an *Ineligible Categories of Employment List*, which includes occupations for which it is not possible to obtain an EP. These are mainly, but not exclusively, low skilled occupations, such as operatives, and service industry personnel. The list also includes a number of more highly skilled professions where skills surpluses have been detected such as physiotherapists.

Before a General EP or a Contract for Services EP can be issued to a non-EEA national, employers must satisfy a labour market lest to assess whether a job could be done by an available EU worker. The test "requires" that the employer advertise the vacancy with the Department of Social Protection Employment Services/EURES employment network for at least 2 weeks. The vacancy has to be announced also in a national newspaper for at least 3 days and in either a local newspaper or jobs website for 3 days.

EPs are not granted to companies unless 50% or more of the employees in the firm are EEA nationals at the time of application. This restriction may be waived for start-up companies within 2 years of their establishment and which are supported by the enterprise development agencies.

Registration Scheme would also provide additional efficiency gains. These efficiency gains would offer some scope to reduce fees, in case the current structure proves to be acting as a barrier for migrants' entry.

The role of return migration

Return migration, i.e. emigrants returning to Ireland, could play a significant role in the recovery of Ireland's economy and in providing skills, relevant working experience and networks. Evidence shows that return migrants bring back skills, networks and financial capital, and can thereby help spur innovation and growth (OECD, 2008a). It can also be an important source of entrepreneurship for Ireland, as a significant proportion of return migrants tend to start a business or arrange independent employment after their return.

Beyond their economic impact, large emigration flows may have psychological and cultural effects on those staying in the country. In particular, international evidence shows that parents can suffer declines in mental health as a result of the emigration of their offspring (Antman, 2010). Emigration has also been found to reduce the happiness of the family left behind, and immigrants tend to be less happy than natives in the destination country (Simpson, 2011). Evidence of mental health declines in mothers and older fathers of emigrants has also been found for Ireland (Mosca and Barrett, 2014).

Return migration rates can be very significant. International evidence shows that between 20% and 50% of immigrants leave within five years after their arrival either to return home or move on to a third country (OECD, 2008a). The return rate does not generally vary much by gender, but it changes sharply over the life cycle of migrants, with higher rates for the young and for retirees. The return rate is higher at the high and low ends of the education spectrum.

Return migration made a positive contribution to the Irish economy in mid-1990s. But now competition for skills is global and fiercer and the return of Irish recent migrants cannot be taken for granted. Canada, the United States, Australia and New Zealand, countries that have recently received significant Irish emigration, have been found to be more successful than European countries in retaining immigrants (OECD, 2008a). In addition, existing communities of Irish emigrants in those countries make it easier for their compatriots to integrate and stay abroad. Emigration has been large in the 25-44 age bracket, an age where people tend to start making longer-term commitments to careers and their location than those in younger cohorts.

There are many factors affecting return migration decisions. Availability of employment is a key factor, although most of the recent emigrants were in employment prior to their departure. Wage and tax differentials as well as housing and childcare affordability may also be key factors. The capacity of the Irish economy to raise its productivity level would determine to which extent Ireland will be able to pay higher wages in the future in a sustainable way. Ireland high public debt entails that tax burden is expected to be high in the coming years. Continuing efforts to reduce public debt would also render medium-term positive effects in making Ireland a more attractive destination for workers by reducing the need to raise taxes in the future.

The increased mobility of high-skilled workers has motivated many OECD countries to use the tax system via preferential schemes to try to attract or retain skilled workers (OECD, 2011). These preferential schemes aim to capture positive knowledge spill-overs (e.g. in Denmark, Finland, Italy, Korea and Sweden), particularly from workers engaged in R&D activities, or at addressing skill shortages.

Tax concessions for high-skilled workers reduce equity to the extent they diminish the progressivity of the tax systems. Other tax solutions might therefore be preferable. A number of countries provide tax exemptions from fringe benefits paid by employers to cover costs purely related to the relocation. Those payments are aimed at offsetting higher expenses that workers face when moving and they do not increase disposable income. Belgium, France, the Netherlands and Switzerland provide these exemptions. Lowering personal income tax rates for the entire population, migrant or not, and shifting towards less mobile bases such as consumption and immovable property may also make a country more tax competitive for high-skilled workers. Such reforms would also have positive effect on growth (Johansson et al., 2008) and, if well targeted, would not hamper the equality of the tax system.

Ireland has currently in place the Special Assignee Relief Programme ("SARP"), a tax relief designed to assist multinational companies in attracting key employees to Ireland. The employee must have been employed overseas by the firm for six months prior to arriving in Ireland and must not have been tax resident in Ireland for any of the five years preceding the arrival. He must have a minimum base salary of EUR 75 000. Then 30% of the employee's salary in excess of EUR 75 000 will be disregarded for income tax purposes. This scheme, which is similar to those available in some other EU countries, has the potential to harm the progressivity of the tax system, and it is not useful for domestic firms that would like to attract overseas talent. The government should consider scrapping it. Instead, tax deductions for expenses incurred in the relocation to Ireland, such as travel costs between the place of residence abroad and Ireland, would be preferable to attract skills, not only to the multinational sector but also to domestic companies, without damaging the progressivity of the tax system. If the employer pays these expenses, he would deduct them from its taxable corporate income. When the costs are borne by the employee, then the employee would benefit from the deduction against the personal taxable income. It would be a one-off deduction at the time of relocation, it would be granted on account of the cost actually incurred, and should be capped in amount.

Connecting with the Irish diaspora

Additional policies that could facilitate a smooth return to Ireland include setting-up systems of information and cultural outreach to expatriate communities. Ireland has explicit and elaborated policies to engage with its emigrants abroad. It has recently formulated its approach in a comprehensive diaspora policy review (DFA, 2015). The number of Irish nationals residing abroad is large and their needs vary from those facing vulnerable situations and in need of support to those requiring return counselling or information about possible job opportunities in Ireland. The Irish diaspora policy review is comprehensive enough to cater for those different requirements and needs. Its full deployment could be facilitated by a more systematic effort to gather information concerning the situation of Irish emigrants residing abroad.

One aspect with significant room for improvement concerns emigrant's political representation and right to vote in Irish elections. Ireland is one of the few countries in Europe not to offer some form of suffrage to its citizens who live abroad (Honohan, 2011). The vast majority of countries have electoral systems allowing emigrants to participate in some ways in elections. Voting can allow states to build and retain highly productive connections with diaspora groups (Collier and Vathi, 2007). Political participation is positively associated with well-being (Frey et al., 2008 and Blais and Gelineau, 2007). Thus, civil and political engagement is one of the building blocks of the OECD's Better Life index. Allowing for the participating of Irish emigrants in domestic electoral process would reinforce their attachment to Ireland, would bolster the linkages that Ireland has been successfully building over the years and would make a positive contribution to emigrant's well-being.

Well-being and the quality of services can attract skills

With many OECD countries competing to attract skills, the overall quality of life and, more generally, a high level of well-being can differentiate Ireland from other competitors. Beyond ensuring a reasonable cost of living, including accommodation, it would entail ensuring good availability of childcare and good quality health and education.

The availability of reasonably priced quality childcare is important to attract families where both partners have careers. Childcare costs in Ireland are the second highest in the OECD for couples. At the same time the quality of childcare services is extremely variable (Hanafin, 2014). Further efforts to ensure a provision of more affordable and higher quality childcare services would contribute to make Ireland more family-attractive. A step in this direction has been taken with the publication of recommendations by the Inter Departmental Group on Future Investment in early years and school age care and education services on these issues.

Workers are also attracted by good quality healthcare services. Citizens are less satisfied with the quality of the healthcare in Ireland than in most of the EU advanced economies (Eurobarometer, 2014). As in other countries, foreign workers face problems to access and traverse the system. Some multinationals have set-up dedicated training for their personnel aimed at helping them navigate the Irish health system. Despite that, foreign workers tend to choose to travel to their countries of origin for their medical treatments when possible. Making the health system easier to access and more reliable would make an important contribution to Ireland's attractiveness.

In the same vein, access to good education is key to attracting workers, for whom it is important to be able to continue their children's education after relocating to another country. In that sense, Ireland has a deficit as concerns the availability of international baccalaureate programmes and of non-denominational school options (UN, 2014). Expanding their availability would be notably valuable in a strategy to make quality of life and services in Ireland an additional reason for workers to choose to move or return to Ireland.

Integrating migrants

Large-scale immigration is a relatively new phenomenon in Ireland. The proportion of foreign-born doubled in the last decade, which is a very rapid increase by OECD standards. Ireland's proportion of foreign-born individuals surpasses now the one observed in countries with long immigration histories such as the United States, United Kingdom, France or Netherlands. An additional distinctive feature of Ireland's immigrant community is that it encompasses very heterogeneous groups, with different challenges and needs. Adequate integration policies are needed to help immigrants adapt to Ireland and to avoid that some of them suffer economic and social disadvantages. How well Ireland succeeds in integrating the recent inflows of immigrants will also have a positive effect on Ireland's attractiveness as a potential destination for migrants.

Ireland receives three broad groups of immigrants: returning Irish emigrants, migrants from other EU countries and migrants from the rest of the world. The first group tend to integrate smoothly into the labour market, but some experience difficulties such as social isolation (Barret and Mosca, 2013). Prior to the recession EU immigrants was largely dominated by workers from EU NMS countries. Those workers tended to be relatively well educated and had a higher activity rate than domestic workers, but tended to have low-skilled low-paid jobs. The challenge for this group is to fully utilise their skill levels, which requires that formal qualifications from their countries of origin be recognised. The "rest of the world group" is rather diverse, and includes skilled migrants entering via work permits, family members of immigrants and Irish nationals, and refugees. The number of refugees is relatively small but they are the most difficult integration challenge.

Immigrants were particularly hit by the crisis

Labour market engagement is the cornerstone of a successful integration. As in other OECD countries, the impact of the crisis has been also severe on immigrants. The increase in the unemployment rate has been larger for immigrants than for native's workers (Figure 2.11, panel A), and the immigrant employment rate has fallen since the recession, declining from 75% to 60%, which is its historical minimum and well below the OECD average (Figure 2.11, panel B). An analysis of labour market transitions in Ireland confirms that non-Irish individuals' likelihood of being unemployed increased sharply during the recession in comparison with Irish workers'. The size of the increase differed across education levels and nationalities, with low-educated and African individuals facing the highest difficulties to regain employment (Kelly et al., 2015).

As strong economic growth strengthens and translates into more job opportunities, it is important to analyse whether the recovery is translating into new jobs also for immigrants and whether any specific group may be facing special difficulties that may

Figure 2.11. **Immigrants were particularly hit by the crisis**

Persons aged 15-64

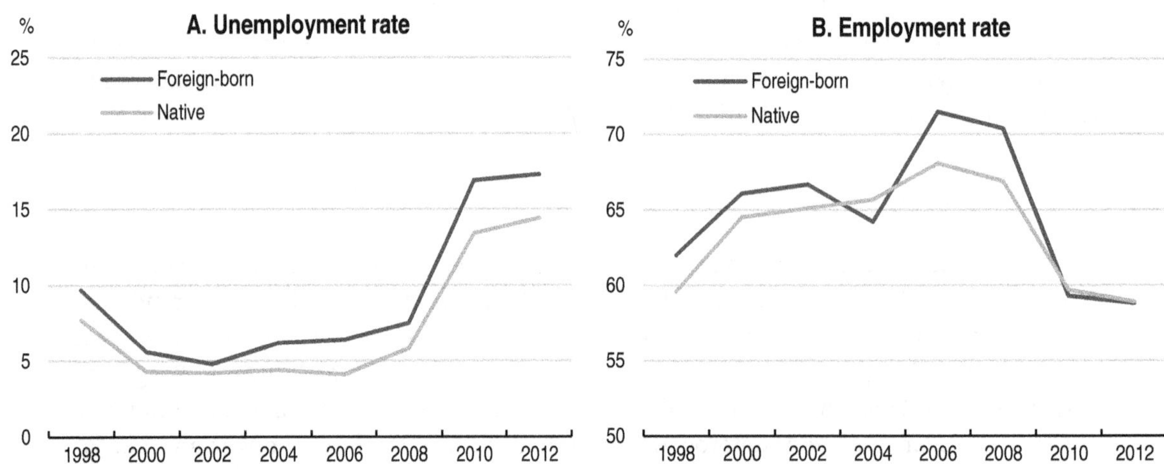

Note: New series from 2006.
Source: Eurostat.

StatLink http://dx.doi.org/10.1787/888933275410

require targeted policy actions. Labour market transition analyses indicate that, as the economy recovers, the gap with respect to Irish nationals in terms of employment probabilities is receding to pre-crisis levels (Kelly et al., 2015). There are notable differences, however, depending on age, education or, especially, length of residence in Ireland. Recently arrived immigrants face employment probabilities similar to Irish workers'. Conversely, longer-resident immigrants' likelihood of unemployment rose over the recession. This suggests that this group of workers may have suffered from scarring effects and highlights the need that they receive assistance and support to increase their employability.

Access to support and activation services by unemployed immigrants are crucial to prevent this group becoming a permanent casualty of the recession and falling into social exclusion. Data on claims by immigrants for unemployment and other employment-related government assistance increased substantially during the recession. Nevertheless the administrative data on the proportions of Irish and non-Irish nationals in receipt of welfare payments, show, so far, no evidence of a large or systematic over-representation of non-Irish nationals among welfare recipients in Ireland (Quinn et al., 2014).

Some ambiguities concerning the accessibility of immigrants to social assistance have been identified and should be addressed. For example, access to most social assistance payments in Ireland requires claimants to meet the "habitual residence" condition. The term "habitual residence" implies "that a person has been here for some time, from a date in the past, and is intending to stay for a period into the foreseeable future" (DSP, 2013). This definition entails a significant degree of subjectivity that complicates ensuring consistency in decision making. A clearer definition of "habitual residence", based on more objective criteria, would facilitate its clear-cut application by caseworkers and provide more certainty to immigrants. There are also additional ambiguities concerning the iterations between immigration and social security policies (Quinn et al., 2014). Eliminating those ambiguities would provide more certainty to both immigrants and government officials concerning entitlements for social assistance and support.

Avoiding a cycle of brain gain, waste and drain

Across the OECD immigrants tend to be at a higher risk of being overqualified than native-born, i.e. they are more likely to be educated beyond what is necessary for a job, especially if they were born in a lower-income country and obtained their highest degree abroad (OECD, 2012). Ireland's immigrants are generally highly educated; however, not all of them are employed in occupations that fully reflect these high education levels. 41% of the tertiary-educated foreign workers have jobs below their formal qualification level (Figure 2.12). This is above percentages observed in other advanced European countries and above the EU average, which stands at thirty-two percent. The high rate in Ireland is primarily driven by nationals of EU NMS countries (Barrett and Duffy, 2007). Conversely, workers from non-EEA countries are less-likely to be overqualified, being its immigration based on working-permits linked with qualifications with high demand.

The prospects of accessing a well-matched job appeared to be strongly related to the field of study, both for foreign-born and native-born (Figure 2.13). Foreign workers with a degree in health are less affected by over-qualification, which may reflect the strong outflow of medical graduates educated in Ireland and relative wage conditions in the sector. Although 20% of them still suffer some degree of miss-matching, this is similar to the rate observed among native-workers. For other fields of study, over-qualification is

Figure 2.12. **Over-qualification and mismatches rates are higher for foreign-born**

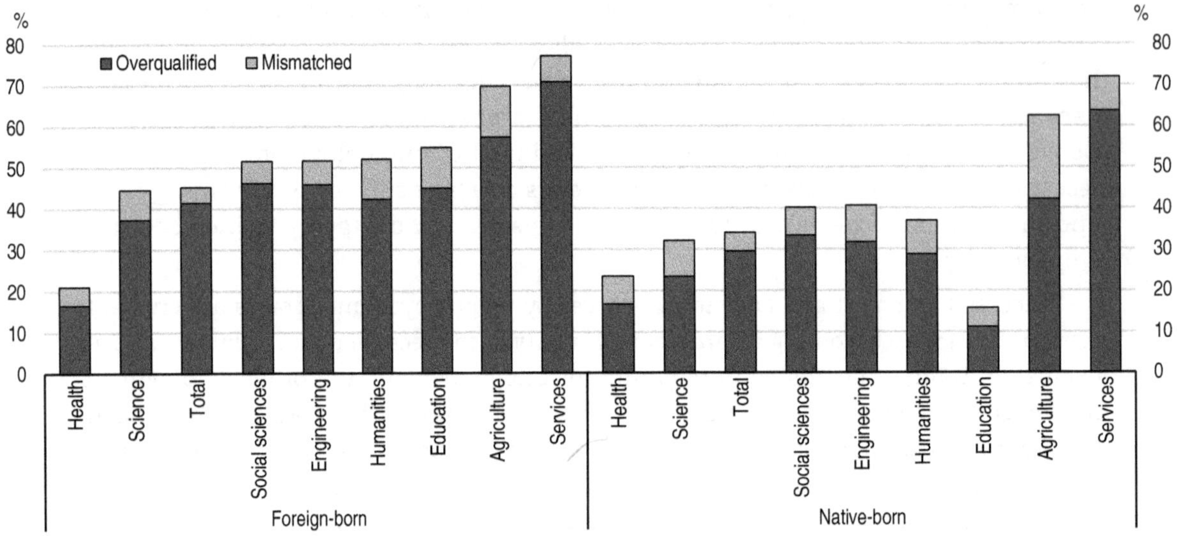

Source: OECD based on European Union Labour Force Survey (Eurostat) data.

StatLink http://dx.doi.org/10.1787/888933275428

Figure 2.13. **Chances of having a well-matched job depend on field of study**

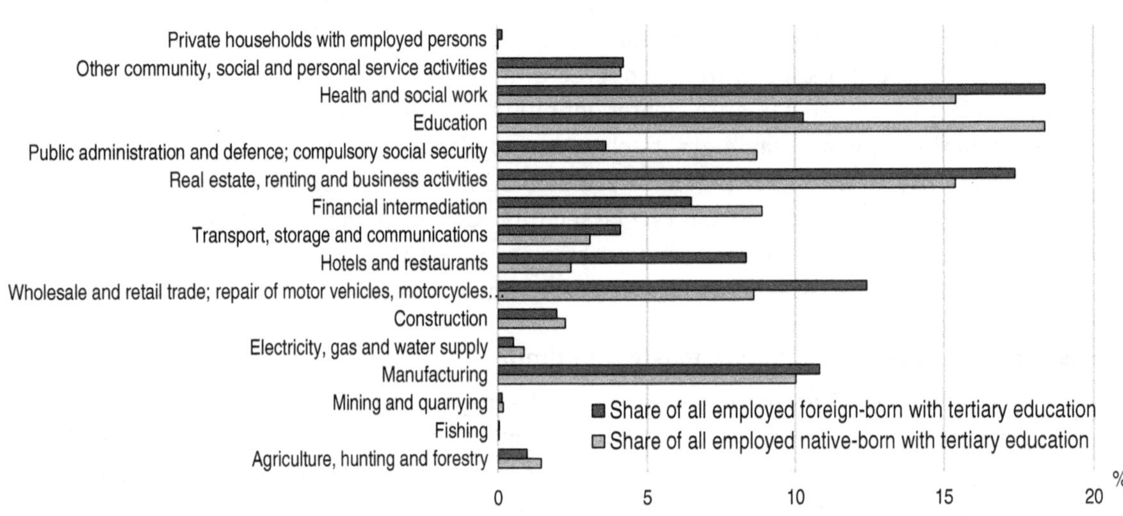

Source: OECD based on Census (2011).

StatLink http://dx.doi.org/10.1787/888933275432

higher among foreign-born workers than for native-born workers. This reflects a high proportion of tertiary educated foreign workers employed in sectors such as hotels and restaurants and also wholesale and retail trade.

High over-qualification rates imply risks of entering a cycle of brain gain, waste and drain, whereby Ireland could be initially successful in attracting highly qualified workers, but they are unable to fully utilise their human capital, which depreciates over time. Eventually those workers are likely to move to a third country or return home. Signs of cycles of brain gain, waste and drain have been observed in Ireland in some sectors such as health (Humphries et al., 2013). Comparable cross-country data on re-emigration rates is scarce, but the existing evidence indicates that re-emigration rates are relatively higher in

Ireland. Workers coming to Ireland tend to leave the country after five years at higher frequency than in other countries (OECD, 2008).

Increasing support for language training for adults, facilitating on the job-training and expediting recognition of professional qualifications gained abroad would contribute to making the most of immigrant workers and would facilitate smoother integration into the Irish labour market. Poor English can partly explain the high over-qualification rates among immigrants, and tend to translate into low-paid jobs. International experience suggests that, across countries, about one third of immigrant over-qualification rates can be explained by weaker linguistic skills (Bonfanti and Xenogiani, 2014). Evidence for Ireland with data prior to the recession confirmed that migrants from English-speaking backgrounds suffered from no earnings gap with respect to natives, while migrants from non-English speaking countries tend to earn a fifth less than comparable natives (Barrett and McCarthy, 2007). More recent data confirms this finding for migrants from EU NMS countries. Despite having a relatively similar educational profile to Irish workers, they disproportionally occupy jobs at the lower level of the occupational ladder and have much lower incomes (Roeder et al., 2014).

Ireland developed a strategy to improve language training for adult immigrants before the recession (OMI, 2008), reflecting that immigrant's ability to speak English was considered a critical and key factor to facilitate immigrant's integration. Nevertheless, fiscal difficulties experienced since then have not allowed the implementation of government strategies in this area (Sheridan, 2015). At the moment there is not a clearly defined strategy for English language training for adults (McGinnity et al., 2014). As more fiscal space becomes available, language training for adult migrants should be increased to help Ireland to get the most out of their immigrant workers.

Another potential barrier for immigrants are difficulties to get foreign qualifications recognised in Ireland. There is clear evidence that qualifications and skills acquired abroad are not transferred swiftly to the Irish labour market and that they translate into pay gaps. These gaps are larger the higher the level of education (Barrett et al., 2012). This suggests that immigrants, and the Irish economy, are not able to obtain a full return on their human capital endowments. This may relate to a lack of location-specific human capital, quality differences between education systems or insufficient knowledge about the quality of foreign qualifications by Irish employers. One way to acquire location-specific skills would be via on-the-job training. Nevertheless, immigrants are also less likely to receive training from employers. Immigrants from EU NMS States experience a particular disadvantage on this front (Barrett et al., 2013). It is critical to ensure a greater participation by immigrants in employer-provided training activities to improve their labour market prospects.

In Ireland recognition of foreign qualifications is facilitated by the state agency *Quality and Qualifications Ireland*. Recognition is made via comparative statements, which offer advice on the recognition of a foreign qualification by comparing it to a level on the National Framework qualifications (NFQ). It takes approximately twelve weeks for an assessment to be completed. The NFQ also provides the possibility for recognising professional qualifications. For the time being, only chartered accountants have made use of that opportunity. Those that have obtained a professional qualification outside Ireland and want to practise need to process the recognition through the relevant professional body. These bodies can act in a protectionist way. As a result, the timeliness, burden, and transparency of the recognition process vary across different professional bodies.

Extending the use of the National Framework Qualifications for professional qualifications would provide a clearer and consistent framework, which would benefit both foreign-born and Irish-born that may have gained a professional qualification abroad and wish to exercise that profession back in Ireland.

Discrimination can also be an important obstacle for labour market integration. Discrimination is difficult to measure and cross-country comparable statistics are sparse. One way to detect and measure discrimination is to use field experiments, particularly "correspondence tests", in which fictitious written applications are sent in response to real job advertisements and discrimination is measured by comparing invitations to interviews among different groups. Most such experiments indicate that discrimination in the hiring process is common (OECD, 2008b). With strictly equivalent qualifications and working experience, international evidence signals that ethnic minorities receive about 30 percentage points less invitations for interview than the rest of the population. Existing evidence for Ireland suggests that discrimination could be even higher, although experiments conducted in different countries are not fully comparable. Thus, job applicants with Irish names are estimated to be over twice as likely to be invited to interview as candidates with identifiably non-Irish names (McGinnity et al., 2009). Workers of black ethnicity have the highest risk of discrimination (McGinnity et al., 2012). Continuing vigilance with respect to possible discrimination practices seems therefore warranted.

Preparing for challenges associated with second generation immigrants

The second generation is large and diverse (Roeder et al, 2014). While its size is smaller than the one found it other OECD countries with a longer history of immigration, the second generation cohort is growing rapidly in Ireland. The share of children born in Ireland from a non-Irish mother was nearly insignificant at the beginning of the previous decade. Now one in four children born in Ireland has a non-Irish born mother. About half of the non-Irish mothers are made up by mothers from EU NMS countries. Children born in Ireland are also of increasingly diverse ethnic and religious backgrounds. Asian and African mothers accounts for 4% and 3% respectively of the total children and this is also growing rapidly. Experience in other countries indicates that integration outcomes among second generation immigrant's communities tend to be closely determined by ethnicity. International experience also suggests that early action is critical to prevent that native-born children of immigrants have lower outcomes than the children of natives and to avoid marginalisation and ghettoisation patterns observed in other countries.

First-generation immigrant students in Ireland, on average, achieve education outcomes similar to their Irish-born peers. However, the integration of second generation immigrants will imply new and additional challenges for the Irish educational system. One of them concerns English language ability, in particular of children from households with parents who do not speak English at home. Language disadvantage tends to occur in such contexts, impacting negatively on school achievement. Indeed, a gap in achievement between those who speak English at home and those who do not has already become apparent (OECD, 2009), especially concerning English reading abilities for 15 year olds (McGinnity et al., 2014). English language support has been merged in the budget with special needs education, which complicates the monitoring of the budget allocation for teaching English as an additional language (McGinnity et al. 2014). Providing students of foreign language background with appropriate English language acquisition support is crucial for the integration of immigrant communities.

Language disadvantages may be amplified by the very low-rate of childcare usage among those households more likely to speak another language at home, such as migrants from EU NMS countries. The cost of preschool childcare in Ireland is high in international perspective. While this affects all segments of Irish population, immigrants are likely to be highly affected, because some of them tend to be of low economic status and are less likely to have family around so they depend more heavily on non-family childcare options. The introduction of the Early Childhood Care and Education (ECCE) Scheme, which provides a free year of early childhood care and education for children of pre-school age, will help in this regard. Similar programs in other countries have been found to particularly benefit migrant communities (Magnuson et al., 2006). The scheme should be evaluated to guarantee that it is well targeted and that it reaches non-English-speaking families in lower income groups. In case of a positive evaluation, extending it beyond one year, particularly for low income groups, should be considered, in line with similar schemes in other countries.

In addition to language disadvantages, it is also crucial to assess the overall situation of immigrants in the educational system, especially concerning how the social background of schools may be affecting educational outcomes. There is evidence in Ireland that the school social mix has a strong effect on educational outcomes (McCoy et al., 2014). Young people from working-class backgrounds are less likely to go on to higher education than their middle-class peers and are also more likely to be unemployed upon leaving school.

In addition, there are also incipient signs that the concentration of immigrant children in primary schools has increased significantly. According to the latest school census, 80% of children from immigrant backgrounds were concentrated in 20% of primary schools. In 15 schools, more than two-thirds of pupils are of non-Irish background. This is partly explained by geographical location of migrant communities. Migrant and minority ethnic students are more likely to be located in urban areas, translating into higher concentration of immigrants in schools in those areas. But admission procedures to schools are also contributing to the increasing concentration. Where there are more applicants than places, selection criteria are up to the schools, which tend to favour children whose parents had been resident in the area for some time. As a result, newer schools have much higher percentages of immigrant children than older schools. International evidence shows that immigrant concentration in disadvantaged schools has a negative effect on educational attainment (Portes and Hao, 2004). Policy options to avert such negative effects include investing more in disadvantaged schools, for example by offering higher teacher pay, reducing class sizes, and providing additional remedial or tutoring help. Another policy option would be to attempt to reduce concentration through school admission policies (OECD, 2012). Admission policies based on who lives nearest may result in excessive concentration of students of low economic background in disadvantaged schools and low chances for them to attend the best schools. An alternative to achieve a higher mix, in terms of socio-economic background, ethnicity and academic ability, would be to explicitly seek for a more diverse composition of students by establishing explicit targets. Another possibility would be to use as a tie-breaker when schools are oversubscribed other criteria than distance, such as a random draw. Both the provision of additional support to disadvantaged schools and changes to school admission policies would be more effective if implemented early on in the school trajectory.

There has been a rapid rise in the size of the naturalised population in the last few years, due to increased applications as well as improvements in the processing of applications This implies that relying exclusively on nationality to monitor the situation of immigrants and guide policies will become increasingly problematic. Ireland does not run immigrant specific surveys, and existing data sources, such as the Quarterly National Household Survey (QNHS) and the Census, have limitations. The definition of an immigrant is often based on nationality, and even though place of birth is recorded in the QNHS, this information is often missing for the non-Irish born, so that official statistics are often exclusively based on nationality, without any information on birthplace (O'Connell and McGinnity, 2008). The QNHS furthermore does not generally include ethnicity questions, with the exception of the equality module, which only give figures for EU NMS countries migrants as a whole, and not for individual countries of origin. Since immigrant integration varies significantly depending on country of origin and ethnicity, improving information available on those dimensions would contribute to better monitoring second immigration integration challenges and to better targeting immigration policies.

Adapting labour market, education and pension policies

Large waves of migration translate into changing population profiles and needs. This highlights the need to continuously adapt labour market and education policies. This requires a more systematic evaluation of policies and programmes, allocating resources to those found to be successful and closing down those no longer effective, as recommended in OECD (2013).

It is important that programmes are implemented to ensure that vulnerable groups are integrated and their skills needs targeted so they can also take part in Ireland's current recovery. Targeted labour market and education programmes that focus on providing equal employment opportunities, and offer retraining, education, and language and cultural supports, are vital for ensuring that legally resident immigrants have an equal chance to participate in the labour market and avoid long-term unemployment. Efforts to ensure that immigrants are able to access the enhanced activation services and improved training opportunities that authorities are deploying should continue.

It is also important to ensure an adequate portability of old-age benefits, and in particular of retirement benefits. This is normally implemented via international social security bilateral agreements. Currently Ireland has bilateral agreements with around 20 countries, including the majority of countries that are traditional destinations of Irish emigrants such as Australia, Canada, New Zealand and the United States. The main purpose of these bilateral agreements is to protect the pension rights of persons who have paid social insurance contributions in Ireland and have accrued pensionable periods in the other country. Reflecting the increasing nationality mix of people residing in Ireland, bilateral agreements with non-EU countries from which Ireland has received significant immigration would be very beneficial and should be pursued. In that sense, OECD countries tend to have bilateral agreements with a large number of countries; Spain has agreements with 140 countries, Canada with 180, Italy with 112, and Portugal with 97.

Recommendations for getting the most out of migration

Maintaining and reinforcing attractiveness for skilled workers

- Increase the use of IT in employment permits processes and of simplified trust-based schemes. Pass the savings on to lower permit fees.
- Ensure that salary thresholds do no act as a barrier for recent graduates. Establish differentiated thresholds for recent graduates in case they do.
- Expand the availability of non-denominational school options and of international baccalaureate programs.

Facilitating that domestic companies also get the most out of labour market openness

- Consider scrapping the Special Assignee Relief Programme, granting tax rebates at multinational executives. Instead, provide tax deductions for relocation expenses incurred when workers move to Ireland.
- Encourage and facilitate that SMEs make use of trusted-based schemes.
- Provide SMEs with specialised support in international recruitment processes.

Connecting with the Irish diaspora

- Increase efforts to gather information on Irish emigrants on a more consistent manner.

Fostering labor market integration of immigrants

- Use the National Framework Qualifications for the recognition of professional qualifications gained abroad.
- Promote greater participation from immigrants in employer-provided training activities.
- Step up targeted language training to adult migrants.
- To guarantee clear-cut access to social assistance by immigrants, establish a clearer definition of "habitual residence" and avoid ambiguous criteria such as "burden on the state".
- Establish bilateral social security agreements with non-EU countries from which Ireland has received significant immigration.

Preparing for challenges associated to second generation immigrants

- Increase availability and access to preschool childcare by immigrants families.
- Adjust school admission policies to avoid excessive concentration of immigrants in disadvantaged schools. Provide additional support to disadvantaged schools.
- Provide students with foreign language backgrounds English language support.
- Improve information available in official statistics concerning immigrant's country of origin and ethnicity.

Building a flexible housing market

Step up efforts to check the compliance with existing quality standards for rental accommodation.

Simplify rental contract legislation.

Bibliography

Antman, Francisca M. (2010), "Adult Child Migration and the Health of Elderly Parents Left Behind in Mexico", *American Economic Review: Papers & Proceedings*, 100: 205-208.

Arslan, C., et al. (2015), "A New Profile of Migrants in the Aftermath of the Recent Economic Crisis",*OECD Social, Employment and Migration Working Papers*, No. 160, OECD Publishing, Paris. doi: *http://dx.doi.org/10.1787/5jxt2t3nnjr5-en*.

Barret, A. and D. Duffy (2007), "Are Ireland's Immigrants Integrating into its Labour Market?,", *ESRI Working Paper*, No.199, Economic and Social Research Institute, Ireland.

Barrett, A., S. McGuinness and M. O'Brien (2012), "The Immigrant Earnings Disadvantage across the Earnings and Skills Distributions: The Case of Immigrants from the EU's New Member States", *British Journal of Industrial Relations*, London School of Economics, Vol. 50(3), pages 457-481, 09.

Barrett, A. and I. Mosca (2013), "Social Isolation, Loneliness and Return Migration: Evidence from Older Irish Adults", *Journal of Ethnic and Migration Studies*, 39:10, 1659-1677, doi: 10.1080/1369183X.2013.833694.

Barrett, A., S. McGuinness, M. O'Brien and P. O'Connell (2013), "Immigrants and Employer-provided Training", *Journal of Labor Research*, Springer, Vol. 34(1), pages 52-78, March.

Barrett, A. and I. Mosca (2014), "The Impact of Adult Child Emigration on the Mental Health of Older Parents", *IZA Discussion Papers*, No. 8037, Institute for the Study of Labor (IZA).

Barrett, A. and Y. McCarthy (2007), "The Earnings of Immigrants in Ireland: Results from the 2005 EU Survey of Income and Living Conditions", *IZA Discussion Papers*, No. 2990.

Blais, A. and F. Gélineau (2007), "Winning, Losing and Satisfaction with Democracy", *Political Studies Volume 55, Issue 2*, pages 425-441, June 2007.

Bonfanti, S. and T. Xenogiani (2014), "Migrants' skills: Use, mismatch and labour market outcomes – A first exploration of the International Survey of Adult Skills (PIAAC)", in OECD and European Union, *Matching Economic Migration with Labour Market Needs*, OECD Publishing, Paris, doi: *http://dx.doi.org/10.1787/9789264216501-11-en*.

Central Bank of Ireland (CBI) (2015), *Central Bank Quarterly Bulletin – 2015 Q2*, April 2015.

Collyer, M. and Z. Vathi (2007), "Patterns of Extra-territorial Voting", *Working Paper*, T22, Sussex Centre for Migration Research.

Conefrey, T. and R. Smith (2014), "On the Slide? Salary Scales for New Graduates 2004-2012", *Economic Letters*, 2014, Vol. 1. Central Bank of Ireland.

Docquier, F. and A. Marfouk (2006), "International Migration by Education Attainment, 1990-2000", in Ç. Özden and M. Schiff (eds.), *International Migration, remittances, and the Brain Drain*, Washington/New York, The World Bank and Palgrave Macmillan, pp. 151-199.

Department of Jobs, Enterprise and Innovation (DJEI) (2014), "Employment Permits Home Page", *www.djei.ie/labour/workpermits/index.htm*.

Department of Social Protection (DSP) (2013), *Habitual Residence Condition Guidelines for Deciding Officers on the determination of Habitual Residence*, Available at *www.welfare.ie/en/Pages/home.aspx*.

Department of Foreign Affairs (DFA) (2015), *Global Irish: Ireland's Diaspora Review*.

DKM Economic consultants (2014), *Future of the Private Rented Sector – Final Report*. Prepared for the Housing Agency on behalf of the Private Residential Tenancies Board".

Duffy, D., John Fitz Gerald and Ide Kearney (2005), "Rising House Prices in an Open Labour Market", *The Economic and Social Review*, vol. 36(3), pages 251-272, Economic and Social Research Institute, Ireland.

Eurobarometer (2014), "Patient safety and quality of care", *Special Eurobarometer*, 411.

Frey, B.S., A. Stutzer, M. Benz, S. Meier, S. Luechinger and C. Benesch (2008), *Happiness: A revolution in economics*. Cambridge, MA: MIT Press

Hanafin, S. (2014), *Report on the Quality of Pre-school Services: Analysis of pre-school inspection reports*. Dublin: Tusla, Child and Family Agency.

Honohan, I. (2011) ", Should Irish Emigrants have Votes? External Voting in Ireland", *Irish Political Studies*, 26:4, 545-561.

Humphries, N., E. Tyrrell, S. McAleese, P. Bidwell, S. Thomas, C. Normand and R. Brugha (2013), "A cycle of brain gain, waste and drain – a qualitative study of non-EU migrant doctors in Ireland", *Human Resources for Health*, 2013, 11:63.

Izquierdo, M., J.F. Jimeno and A. Lacuesta (2015), "Spain: from immigration to emigration". *Documentos de Trabajo*, No. 1503. Banco de España.

Johansson, A., C. Heady, J. Arnold, B. Brys and L. Vartia (2008), "Taxation and Economic Growth", *OECD Economics Department Working Papers*, No. 620, OECD Publishing, *http://dx.doi.org/10.1787/241216205486*.

Kelly, E., S. McGuinness, P. O'Connell, A. González Pandiella and D. Haugh (2015), "How Well Does Ireland Integrate Migrants into its Labour Market?", *OECD Economics Department Working Papers*, forthcoming.

McCoy, S., E. Smyth, D. Watson and M. Darmody (2014), "Leaving School in Ireland: A Longitudinal Study of Post School Transitions", *ESRI Research Series*, No. 36, Economic and Social Research Institute, Ireland.

McGinnity, F., E. Quinn, G. Kingston and P. O'Connell (2014), *Annual Monitoring Report on Integration 2013*, Dublin: Economic and Social Research Institute and The Integration Centre.

McGinnity, F., D. Watson and G. Kingston (2012), *Analysing the Experiences of Discrimination in Ireland: Evidence from the QNHS Equality Module 2010*, The Equality Authority and the Economic and Social Research Institute, Ireland.

McGinnity, F., J. Nelson, P. Lunn and E. Quinn (2009), *Discrimination in Recruitment – Evidence from a Field Experiment*,The Equality Authority and the Economic and Social Research Institute, Ireland.

Magnuson, K., C. Lahaie and J. Waldfogel (2006), "Preschool and school readiness of children of immigrants", *Social Science Quarterly*, 87(5):1241-62.

Office of the Minister for Integration and the Department of Education & Science Development (OMI) (2008), *A National English Language Policy and Framework for Legally-Resident Adult Immigrants – final report*.

O'Connell, P. and F. McGinnity (2008), *Immigrants at Work. Ethnicity and Nationality in the Irish Labour Market*. Dublin: The Equality Authority/The Economic and Social Research Institute.

OECD (2014a), *International Migration Outlook 2014*, OECD Publishing, *http://dx.doi.org/10.1787/migr_outlook-2014-en*.

OECD (2014b), *Recruiting Immigrant workers: New Zealand*, OECD Publishing, *http://dx.doi.org/10.1787/9789264215658-en*.

OECD (2013), *OECD Economics Survey: Ireland*, 2013, OECD Publishing, *http://dx.doi.org/10.1787/eco_surveys-irl-2013-en*.

OECD (2012), "PISA Untapped Skills: Realising the Potential of Immigrant Students", OECD Publishing, *http://dx.doi.org/10.1787/9789264172470-en*.

OECD. (2011), "The Taxation of Mobile High-Skilled Workers," Chapter 4 in *OECD Tax Policy Study* No. 21: Taxation and Employment, OECD, Paris.

OECD (2009), "OECD Reviews of Migrant Education: Ireland", December 2009. OECD, Paris, *http://dx.doi.org/10.1787/9789264086203-en*.

OECD (2008a), *International Migration Outlook 2008*, OECD Publishing, *http://dx.doi.org/10.1787/migr_outlook-2008-en*.

OECD (2008b), "Ending Job Discrimination", *OECD Policy Brief*, July 2008, Paris, OECD.

Portes, A. and L. Hao (2004), "The Schooling of Children of Immigrants: Contextual Effects on the Educational Attainment of the Second Generation", *Proceedings of the National Academy of Sciences*, 101 (August): 11920-11927.

Quinn, E., E. Gusciute, A. Barrett and J. Corona (2014), "Migrant Access to Social Security and Healthcare: Policies and Practice in Ireland", *ESRI Research Series*, No. 261, Economic and Social Research Institute, Ireland.

Roeder, A., M. Ward, C. Frese and E. Sánchez (2014), "New Irish Families: A Profile of Second Generation Children and their Families", Dublin, Trinity College Dublin, July, 2014.

Simpson, N. (2011), "Happiness and migration", Chapter in *International Handbook on the Economics and Migration*.

Sheridan, V. (2015), "English everywhere and nowhere – ESOL policies in Ireland", Chapter in *Adult Language Education and Migration Challenging agendas in policy and practice*. Edited by James Simpson and Anne Whiteside, Routledge.

United Nations (2014), "Concluding Observations with respect to Ireland's Fourth Periodic Examination under International Covenant on Civil and Political Rights", Human Rights Committee, August, 2014.

Westmore, B. (2014), "International migration: The relationship with economic and policy factors in the home and destination country", *OECD Economics Department Working Papers*, No. 1140, OECD Publishing, *http://dx.doi.org/10.1787/5jz123h8nd7l-en*.

© OECD 2015

ANNEX

Estimation of bilateral migration flows

Equations

$$\textbf{Emigration}: \log(E_t^{DD}) = c + b * \log(E_{t-1}^{DD}) + d^* (UNR_t^{DD} - UNR_t^{IRL})$$

where E_t^{DD} is the emigration from Ireland to country of destination DD in time t, UNR_{IRL} is the unemployment rate in Ireland and UNR_{DD} is the unemployment rates in country destination DD.

	United Kingdom	United States	EU13[1]	Other countries
c	1.176 ***	0.93 ***	0.484 ***	0.718 ***
b	0.447 ***	0.264	0.221	0.669 ***
d	-0.086 ***	-0.052 ***	-0.039 ***	0.006
R-squared	0.87	0.52	0.69	0.92
Durbin-Watson	1.52	1.96	2.29	1.86

$$\textbf{Immigration}: \log(M_t^{OO}) = c + b^* \log(M_{t-1}^{OO}) + d^* (UNR_t^{OO} - UNR_t^{IRL})$$

where M_t^{OO} is the immigration from country OO to Ireland . UNR_{DD} is the unemployment rates in OO.

	United Kingdom[1]	United States	EU13[1]	Other countries[2]
c	2.09 ***	2.405 ***	1.10 ***	1.73 ***
b	0.419 ***	0.474 ***	0.353 ***	0.658 ***
d	0.038 ***	0.0626 ***	0.031 ***	0.073***
R-squared	0.81	0.59	0.76	0.97
Durbin-Watson	2.01	1.65	2.20	1.76

*** significant at 0.05% level
1. Equation includes a linear time trend.
2. Equation includes a dummy variable to capture the effect of accession to the EU of Central and Eastern Europe member states.

The sample covers 1988-2014. The lagged dependent variable captures dynamics of adjustment while the constant c (and trend when included) absorbs other omitted factors. The equations are estimated individually for each destination or country of origin. This is not a full structural model of migration and the results should be interpreted as a reduced form relationship between unemployment rates and bilateral migratory flows. EU13 comprises Austria, Belgium, Denmark, Finland, France, Germany, Greece, Italy,

Luxembourg, Netherlands, Spain, Sweden and Portugal. "Other countries" include all other countries apart from United States, United Kingdom and those not included in EU13. For the "Other countries" category the OECD unemployment rate is used to gauge labour market developments.

ORGANISATION FOR ECONOMIC CO-OPERATION AND DEVELOPMENT

The OECD is a unique forum where governments work together to address the economic, social and environmental challenges of globalisation. The OECD is also at the forefront of efforts to understand and to help governments respond to new developments and concerns, such as corporate governance, the information economy and the challenges of an ageing population. The Organisation provides a setting where governments can compare policy experiences, seek answers to common problems, identify good practice and work to co-ordinate domestic and international policies.

The OECD member countries are: Australia, Austria, Belgium, Canada, Chile, the Czech Republic, Denmark, Estonia, Finland, France, Germany, Greece, Hungary, Iceland, Ireland, Israel, Italy, Japan, Korea, Luxembourg, Mexico, the Netherlands, New Zealand, Norway, Poland, Portugal, the Slovak Republic, Slovenia, Spain, Sweden, Switzerland, Turkey, the United Kingdom and the United States. The European Union takes part in the work of the OECD.

OECD Publishing disseminates widely the results of the Organisation's statistics gathering and research on economic, social and environmental issues, as well as the conventions, guidelines and standards agreed by its members.

OECD PUBLISHING, 2, rue André-Pascal, 75775 PARIS CEDEX 16
(10 2015 17 1 P) ISBN 978-92-64-24032-2 – 2015

www.ingramcontent.com/pod-product-compliance
Lightning Source LLC
LaVergne TN
LVHW081412110826
845149LV00010B/1719
* 9 7 8 9 2 6 4 2 4 0 3 2 2 *